Create Your Own
CROSS STITCH

Create Your Own
CROSS STITCH

How to turn your design ideas into reality

SHIRLEY WATTS

MEREHURST

For Aunty Lilian, who shares my love of flowers,
birds and all other wild creatures. Her courage and
determination to regain mobility after her accident
have been an inspiration to us all.

IMPORTANT NOTICE
All the designs in this book have been stitched with
DMC threads. The keys list the colours used and show
equivalent shades in Anchor and Madeira, or, where
appropriate, Danish Flower threads. The range of
shades differs slightly in each brand, however, and you
may also find that where two very close shades of DMC
have been used it has sometimes been necessary to give
the same shade for both in another brand.

Published in 1993 by Merehurst Limited
Ferry House, 51-57 Lacy Road, Putney, London SW15 1PR

ISBN 1-85391-305-7

A catalogue record for this book is available from the British Library.

Managing editor Heather Dewhurst
Edited by Diana Lodge
Designed by Maggie Aldred
Photography by Lucy Mason, except for pictures on pages 52, 70, 73, 82, 83,
84, 88, 90, 111, 118 and 122, which were provided by Shirley Watts
Typesetting by BMD Graphics, Hemel Hempstead
Colour separation by Fotographics Ltd, London – Hong Kong
Printed in Italy by New Interlitho, S.p.A., Milan

· CONTENTS ·

6
Introduction

8
Basic tools

10
Leaf designs

22
Nuts and mushrooms

38
Autumn berries

46
Garden flowers

66
Pets

80
Wild animals

92
Birds and butterflies

114
Widening your horizons

126
Basic stitches

127
Index

128
Acknowledgements
Suppliers

· INTRODUCTION ·

My first encounter with cross stitch was in 1956 when, as a teenager, I visited Austria with a school party. We spent some time in Innsbruck and there I discovered some beautifully worked cross stitch embroideries in a shop window. How I made myself understood I cannot remember, but I came out of that shop triumphantly clutching hand-drawn patterns of several of the traditional designs. When I got home I meticulously worked them – the biggest project of all being a broad embroidered band, stitched in white thread around the bottom of a red dress. Thus began my fascination with cross stitch.

Cross stitch designs have been devised and embroidered the world over for centuries. Though the basic stitch has remained the same, and though certain geometric and pictorial motifs can be traced from one geographical area to another, each region of the world has its own recognizable style and each generation has developed its own interpretation of traditional themes.

In my own work, inspiration has come largely from nature – from the flowers, animals and insects which flourish in my native Britain. This source of inspiration I share with generations of designers who have gone before me, but it is in the interpretation of the subjects that I hope my designs are distinctively my own. Many of my designs originate as drawings taken from my wildlife photographs. Well-exposed photographs capture the true colours and realistic forms of flowers, fruits and seeds, while many wild birds, animals and insects are so elusive that the only way to capture a true likeness is on film. Creating a three-dimensional image and the illusion of movement in cross stitch designs can only be achieved by accurate observation and the careful choice of colour to pick out light and shade.

Faithful interpretation of colour is often difficult to achieve with the ordinary six-stranded embroidery cottons. Many is the time I have picked a leaf or a flower from the hedgerow and failed to match the colours against my stranded cottons. For this reason I have, in some cases, used Flower Threads. Their matte finish and subtle shades make them ideal for the embroidery of delicately-coloured flowers, fruits and foliage.

In some of my designs I have used metallic blending filaments, to create the illusion of sunlight on water, for example, moonlight on frost, the iridescence of a bird's feathers, or just to evoke a magical quality in my work.

I have had no formal training in embroidery, art or design, and much of my adult life has been devoted to teaching Geography and Geology. The most valuable tuition I received came from my parents. From a very early age my father taught me to draw from life. He taught me to observe, and record carefully, both shape and form, and the patterns of light and shade on my subjects. He also taught me about scale and perspective. As soon as I was old enough he showed me how to use a camera and explained the mysteries of film speed, exposure and composition. My mother taught me to use a needle proficiently, and made sure that I could not only do plain sewing, but could also practise a whole range of decorative handicraft skills. Having said this, however, I must emphasize that no artistic ability is absolutely necessary. Just begin with a few simple ideas and with practice there is no limit to what you can achieve.

It is, perhaps, because of my unorthodox training that many of my methods are unconventional. I prefer to use an ordinary sewing needle for my cross stitch. I do not find that tapestry needles are any more likely to pierce the evenweave fabric through the appropriate hole than a carefully handled sewing needle. I also find that a blunt tapestry needle will not easily pass through the threads at the back of the embroidery when finishing off, especially if the work is fine. My other peculiarity is that I never use an embroidery hoop or frame. I find them cumbersome, and they can so easily snag or leave stretch marks in the material. Like the traditional Icelandic tapestry workers, I like to feel the material scrunched in my hand. As long as your fingers are clean and grease-free, it only needs a good iron to press the crispness back into the work when it is finished.

In planning the projects for this book, I have started with some very simple ideas, for which you will require neither drawing skills nor any knowledge of photography to accomplish an original design. The early part of the book deals with basic skills. From the section about Garden Flowers onwards, the projects are not progressively more difficult, but seek to introduce new ideas, new techniques and new subjects, which I hope will have a wide appeal. If you have never tried to design your own cross stitch, then perhaps now is the time. The satisfaction of producing and working your designs is both exciting and rewarding.

Happy stitching!

Shirley Watts

· BASIC TOOLS FOR DESIGNING ·

Further information about fabrics, threads and camera equipment is given later in this book. What follows here is a simple list of the design tools used when making cross stitch patterns.

Plain drawing paper, HB pencils, pencil sharpener and soft rubber
The first stage in creating a design involves making a sketch of your subject. I always keep a good supply of cheap drawing paper, both for experiments and for drafting very simple designs. I use HB pencils, which are best for this sort of drawing, and I always have a pencil sharpener and soft rubber handy.

Watercolour pad and paints
For more complex subjects, when time permits, a watercolour painting of the design is a useful beginning. A small box of good quality watercolours and two or three artists' brushes are adequate for this purpose.

Camera
A simple camera, capable of taking close-ups, is a useful tool. In addition, some form of storage for your photographs is necessary, to enable you to keep your collection of reference photographs separate from all your other photographs.

Flower press
I have a small flower press which I take on holiday with me, and a larger one which I use at home.

Acetate sheets
It is almost impossible to trace from photographs using ordinary tracing paper. Acetate sheets allow you to see all the detail clearly. You will need overhead projector pens to draw on them. The permanent ones are less messy and do not smudge, but the non-permanent, water-soluble variety are more economical to use because you can wipe off your design and reuse the acetate.

Transparent graph paper
This tracing paper, which has a grid printed on it, is becoming more widely available, in an increasing variety of grid sizes. You can now buy transparent graph paper to match the count of the material for which you are designing – 11, 14, 16, 18, or 22, for example – enabling you to produce a pattern exactly the same size as the finished worked design. This has its advantages, but for the higher counts the squares are extremely tiny, and it is difficult to add symbols or even coloured dots comfortably. I like the traditional size, with 10 squares to 2.5cm (1in), but it is a matter of personal preference.

Calculator

This is useful for calculating the finished size of your design when worked on different counts.

Graph paper

By putting a sheet of plain paper behind your transparent graph paper, you can work directly from the grid, but if you want to store your design, it is more satisfying to transfer it neatly to graph paper. If you want to take up designing more seriously, you may, in time, wish to invest in a computer. There are now several computer-aided cross stitch design programmes on the market, written for a variety of computers.

Ruler, protractor, pair of compasses

You may want to create designs of a variety of shapes and sizes, and for a variety of purposes.

You will find that a simple geometry set is an essential piece of equipment.

Threads

As you do more and more stitching and designing, your collection of six-stranded threads will grow. Always be ready to try out new types of embroidery thread. The uses of Flower Threads and metallic threads are explored in this book.

Needles

For cross stitching on evenweave materials, blunt-ended tapestry needles are recommended. These are available in sizes 18-26.

Scissors

For cutting material you will need sharp dressmaker's shears. For cutting embroidery threads, a pair of small sharp-pointed embroidery scissors or snips is essential.

Materials

If you are a beginner, you will find that cream or white 14-count Aida is a good versatile material to start on. As you become more adventurous you will no doubt want to experiment on different colours and counts, and your stock of materials will grow accordingly.

Lighting

A good clear light is essential if you are to protect your eyesight during long periods of stitching. A magnifying lamp is invaluable for fine work. For dull days and evening sewing, I find 'daylight' bulbs very useful.

For detailed instructions, with diagrams, explaining how to make the basic stitches – cross stitch, backstitch and three-quarter stitch – used in this book, refer to page 126.

*L*EAF
DESIGNS

Creating a simple design taken from nature is a
good way to begin devising your own original
cross stitch patterns. Before you say 'But I
cannot draw', try the following experiments
with autumn leaves. A single leaf can be used
to produce an attractive repeat design, which
might be embroidered on a guest towel. With a
few leaves of varying shapes and colours
you can create a more complex design for a
table place setting.

· A SIMPLE LEAF DESIGN ·

· PREPARATION ·

Collect a range of leaves, selecting those that are perfect and have an interesting shape. Place the leaves between sheets of blotting paper, adding thick layers of newspaper between the blotting paper sandwiches to separate any that have thick stems. Heavy books will press your leaves adequately, but a flower press will press evenly, yielding better results.

———

· YOU WILL NEED ·

A perfectly pressed leaf, measuring approximately 7.5cm (3in) square • Plain white paper • Drawing board or flat surface • An HB pencil • A fine black fibre-tip pen, and a felt-tip pen in the colour of the chosen leaf • Graph tracing paper, with 10 squares to 2.5cm (1in) • Graph paper, with 10 squares to 2.5cm (1in) • Two shades of six-stranded embroidery cotton (to match leaf and leaf veins) • 15cm (6in) square of 14-count Aida fabric • 12.5cm (5in) square of iron-on interfacing • No26 tapestry needle (or any needle with which you feel comfortable)

Note The squares of the graph paper are sufficiently large for symbols (if any) to fit comfortably inside them. If you cannot buy graph tracing paper locally, photocopy a piece of suitable graph paper onto tracing paper. A photocopy agency will do this for you.

1 Take the leaf and lay it on the plain paper. Using the leaf as a template, draw carefully around the shape with a sharp pencil.

2 Remove the leaf and go over the outline with a fine black fibre-tip pen. Carefully draw the stalk and the main veins of the leaf, using the original to ensure that they are true to life.

Select two shades from your range of embroidery cottons, one to match the dominant colour of your leaf, and another for the veins and stalk.

3 Place a piece of graph tracing paper over the leaf outline and tape it down. Draw around the leaf shape, following the outline as closely as possible, but moving only along the vertical and horizontal lines of the graph squares. Mark in the leaf veins, this time either running along vertical and horizontal lines, as before, or moving diagonally across single, double or triple squares. Again, follow the original lines as faithfully as possible.

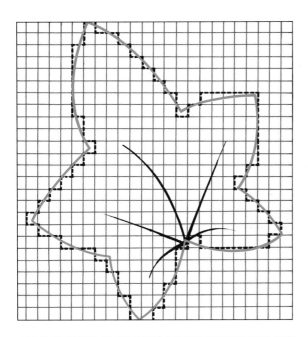

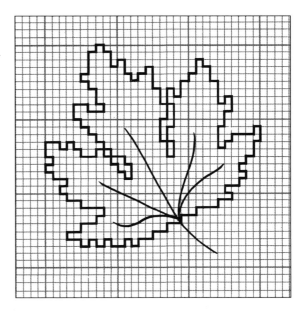

Draw the leaf outline, using graph tracing paper; place the drawing over white paper; transfer it to normal graph paper, and colour in the outline.

An ivy leaf outline has been covered with a sheet of graph tracing paper. If you find it difficult to convert a more complex leaf into a satisfactory graph outline, start with a more simple shape, such as this.

4 Detach your transparent graph paper pattern from the leaf outline and lay it over a piece of plain paper so that you can see the lines clearly. Copy the graph tracing paper outline onto ordinary graph paper. With a felt-tip pen, colour in all the squares that will be covered by cross stitches. Using the black pen, transfer the leaf veins and stalk onto your coloured pattern. These lines will be worked in backstitch.

5 Embroider your leaf motif in the bottom left-hand corner of the Aida fabric, leaving a 2.5cm (1in) border below and to the left of the motif. Centre the interfacing on the back of the fabric and iron it in place. Machine straight stitch around the fabric, 12mm (½in) from the edge. Remove fabric threads below the stitched line on all sides to make the fringe.

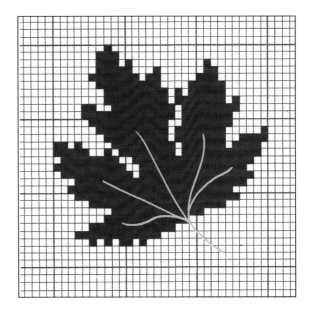

KEY		
Anchor	**Madeira**	**DMC**
310	2009	434 Brown
		Backstitch
362	2012	437 Light brown

· DEVELOPING THE THEME ·

This simple pattern, again based on the leaf outline already shown but with colour shading introduced, might be worked as a motif on any article of your choice or repeated along the edge of a guest towel, tablemat, tablecloth or kitchen curtain – the possibilities are endless.

———

· YOU WILL NEED ·

The basic leaf pattern from the previous project and the original pressed leaf • Three complementary shades of six-stranded embroidery cotton, and one contrast shade for the stalk and veins • An HB pencil and fine black fibre-tip pen • A small guest towel, 45cm × 29cm (18in × 11½in), see page 128 for suppliers

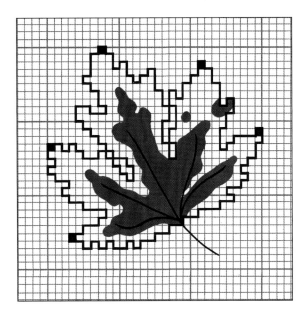

KEY

Anchor	Madeira	DMC	
380	1913	839	Dark brown
365	2010	435	Ginger brown
310	2009	434	Brown

1 Lay your completed leaf pattern from the previous project beside the original pressed leaf. No two leaves are exactly alike, so you have created your own design, but this is only a silhouette. Few leaves are an overall even shade of one colour, and you can make your leaf design more realistic by introducing additional colours.

When I studied my silver maple leaf I observed that there were two browns – a lighter shade around the margins of the leaf and a darker brown adjacent to the veins. The five extreme tips of the leaf were even darker. Take your pattern and sketch, as accurately

as possible, lines separating the different areas of colour on your leaf. On natural objects, such as leaves, colours grade almost imperceptibly one into another, so you can only hope to achieve an approximate division.

2 Indicating the different colours with symbols, fill all the squares of your original silhouette design. Mark arrows at the outer edge to indicate the centre of the design.

Using the motif

To embroider your leaf motif along the bottom of the hand towel, count the squares across the evenweave inset and divide the strip into four equal areas. Mark out each with basting stitches.

Check that your leaf design is of a suitable size to fit into one of these squares – a slightly larger leaf than mine would still fit, but a smaller design might need to be repeated more times to fill the strip adequately. Leaves placed in a slanting position can be arranged more closely together, in which case you might take the precaution of drawing your repeat design on a long piece of graph paper before you begin stitching – it would be annoying to finish up with half a leaf at the side of the towel.

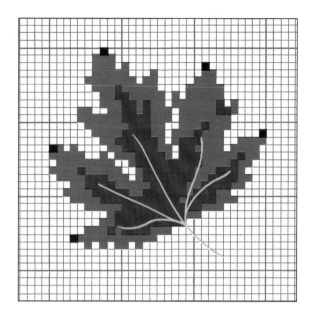

KEY

Anchor	Madeira	DMC
310	2009	434 Brown
365	2010	435 Ginger brown
380	1913	839 Dark brown
		Backstitch
362	2012	437 Light brown

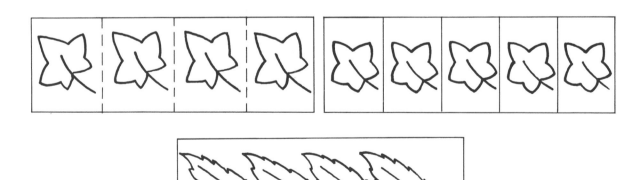

Simple motifs can be repeated as often as required; slanting leaves overlap, however, and you must make allowances for this when calculating how many repeats you will need.

· A LEAFY SPRAY ·

For a more interesting and varied design, you might experiment with a selection of leaves. The design seen here was embroidered on a tablemat, and this idea could be extended by extracting a single leaf from the pattern and using it for complementary sets of glass mats, napkins or fabric napkin holders. The tablemat itself can be finished off in a number of ways: by turning a narrow hem, by making a fringed edge, or by either single or double hem stitching. The one shown here has been completed with single hem stitching.

· YOU WILL NEED ·
Six or seven of your most attractive pressed leaves • An A4 sheet of plain white paper • Drawing board or flat surface • An HB pencil and a fine black fibre-tip pen • Graph tracing paper, with 10 squares to 2.5cm (1in) • Graph paper, with 10 squares to 2.5cm (1in) • Six-stranded embroidery cottons in an appropriate range of shades • 42.5cm × 32.5cm (17in × 13in) of 14-count Aida fabric • No26 tapestry needle (or any needle with which you feel comfortable

1 Arrange your leaves on the paper. If they vary a lot in size, you will find that it looks attractive to place the smaller ones at the top and the larger, heavier leaves towards the bottom. If you are new to design, it would be best to avoid overlapping the leaves, but as you become more confident, you may wish to try out a design with overlapping leaves of various different colours.

2 When you are satisfied with your arrangement, use a sharp HB pencil to draw around each leaf. Begin at the bottom, and remove each leaf when you have finished outlining, to avoid damaging it. Go over the outlines with the black fibre-tip pen, and then draw in the stalks and leaf veins, copying those of the actual leaves as closely as possible.

Sketch in the boundaries between any colour changes that you observe on individual leaves. Use a colour shade card to match the leaf colours to appropriate shades of six-stranded embroidery cotton, pencilling in the selected shade numbers on your drawing.

3 Continue as for the preceding leaf designs until you have the outline on ordinary graph paper.

For a more complex design of this type, you may wish to combine colours with symbols on your chart, or you may opt to use symbols only. Colours are ideal, provided your range of felt-tip pens includes the correct number of clearly identifiable shades, but this is not generally the case. If your embroidery is to feature several shades of green, for example, the chart will be clearer if you either superimpose symbols on the various colours or, alternatively, use symbols only.

In the latter case, choose symbols such as **x**

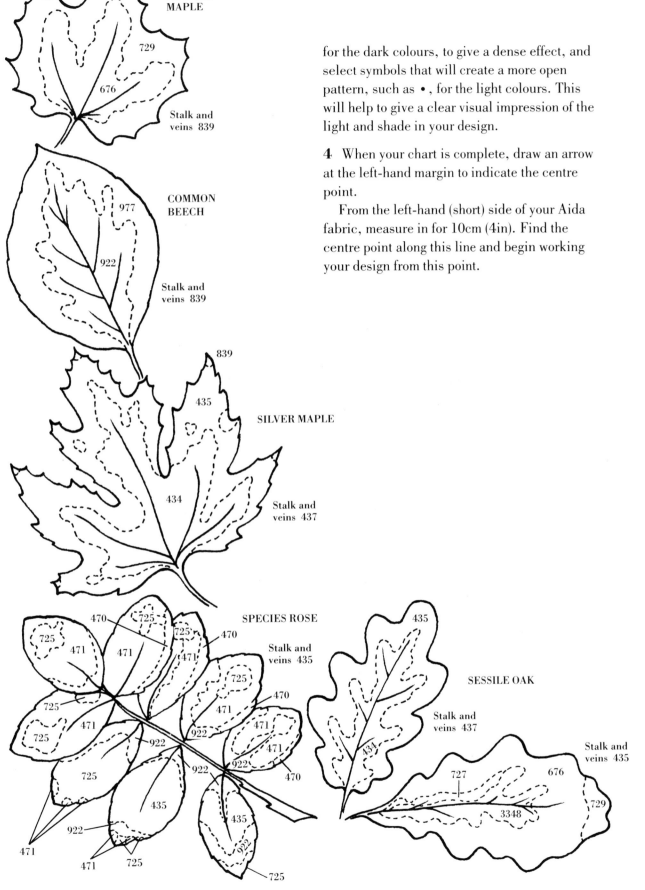

for the dark colours, to give a dense effect, and select symbols that will create a more open pattern, such as •, for the light colours. This will help to give a clear visual impression of the light and shade in your design.

4 When your chart is complete, draw an arrow at the left-hand margin to indicate the centre point.

From the left-hand (short) side of your Aida fabric, measure in for 10cm (4in). Find the centre point along this line and begin working your design from this point.

NORWAY MAPLE

729

676

Stalk and veins 839

COMMON BEECH

977

922

Stalk and veins 839

839

435

SILVER MAPLE

434

Stalk and veins 437

SPECIES ROSE

470   725

725   725   470

725   471   471   471

471   725

725   470

471   471

725   471   922   922   471

922   471

725   922   470

922

471   435   922

922

471   725

725

SESSILE OAK

435

Stalk and veins 435

Stalk and veins 437

434

Stalk and veins 435

727   676

3348   729

LEAVES ▲		ANCHOR	DMC	MADEIRA
✂	Lemon	293	727	0110
I	Deep yellow	297	725	0108
—	Light orange	313	977	2301
Y	Orange	324	922	0310
⊥	Pale green	264	3348	1409
◙	Green	265	471	1501
+	Dark green	266	470	1502
·	Pale fawn	891	676	2208
✤	Fawn	890	729	2209

	Light brown*	362	437	2012
⊦	Ginger brown	365	435	2010
✕	Brown	310	434	2009
⊔	Dark brown	380	839	1913

Backstitching

Light brown* used for backstitch only. Backstitch as follows: Norway maple (Acer platanoides) and common beech (Fagus sylvatica) in dark brown, species rose and yellow-green leaf of sessile oak (Quercus petraea) in ginger brown, and silver maple (Acer saccharinum) and brown leaf of sessile oak in light brown.

Nuts and Mushrooms

To create the illusion of three dimensions on a
flat surface, you need to reproduce, as
faithfully as possible, the patterns of light and
shade upon an object. By drawing acorns,
beechnuts and a few leaves, it is possible to
create a simple working sketch, complete
with highlights and shaded areas,
from which you can embroider a truly
three-dimensional motif.

· DRAWING SIMPLE NATURAL OBJECTS ·

The previous section dealt with pressed leaves, but flowers, fruits, birds and animals are of course three-dimensional, and I am often asked how this effect can be achieved in designs.

Fortunately, the techniques used to create the illusion of a solid object on a flat surface are the same in cross stitch as they are in any other medium, whether it be pencil sketching, water colours, oils or engraving. The key to success lies in careful observation of the patterns of light and shade upon the surface of an object, and transferring these patterns to your design.

The spectacle case design was taken from a number of small acorns and some oak leaves, drawn following the leaf technique describer earlier.

———

• Y O U   W I L L   N E E D •
Drawing materials and graph papers, as described on page 12.

For the spectacle case:
25cm × 15cm (10in × 6in) of 14-count cream Aida fabric • Cream lining fabric – 19cm × 15cm (7½in × 6in) for the front, and two pieces 23cm × 15cm (9in × 6in) for the back • Buckram – 16.5cm × 10cm (6½in × 4in) for the front, and 18cm × 10cm (7in × 4in) for the back • 80cm (32in) of pale brown piping cord, 3mm (⅛in) in diameter • Stranded embroidery cottons, in the colours listed in the panel on page 27

A simple outline of the acorn

1 If you have no previous experience of drawing, or lack confidence, begin with a very simple object, such as an acorn. Draw the outline on paper, trying to get the proportions as accurate as possible. At this stage the acorn still appears flat, as it would if you were to embroider it one shade of acorn brown.

Light and shadow on the acorn

2 Where the surface of the nut slopes away from the light source, it will be in shadow, and therefore a darker shade – the further away from the light, the darker the shadow. On your outline drawing, shade in the dark areas around the edge of the acorn, gradually reducing the depth of shading as you come to the area facing towards you. Your acorn should begin to look solid and rounded.

3 Any shiny object, whether it be an acorn, an apple or the eye of a bird or animal, has highlights where the light is reflected from the

Introducing
the
highlight

surface, so to complete your acorn you must add a highlight. The shape of the highlight will depend upon the form of the object; in this particular case it is a crescent, following the shape of the acorn.

Simplifying
the
shading

4 Place your graph tracing paper over your drawing, and trace onto it the outline of the acorn, following the vertical and horizontal lines, as shown on page 13. Now fill in the squares covering the areas in deep shade, using a symbol appropriate to a dark colour, for example **c**. Fill in the lighter areas with a less dense symbol, such as **+**. Finally, put small dots in each square over the highlighted area, and a different symbol in the squares over the acorn cup.

This is as much detail as you could hope to get on a small motif on this scale. If, however, you drew your acorn twice this size, you could introduce more depth into the shading by recognizing dark, medium and lightly shaded areas, as well as the highlight.

Transfering
the shapes
to graph
paper

- ⊡ Ecru
- **c** Brown
- ⊠ Light brown
- ◣ Purplish brown

Making the case

When you have completed the cross stitching, turn the edges of the Aida fabric over the piece of buckram cut for the front; fold in the front lining and hem it neatly to the edges. Repeat for the back, with the buckram sandwiched between the two pieces of lining material. Seam the back and front together with fine oversewing, and slipstitch a length of cord across the lower front edge and about 12mm (½in) down each side, and the remainder all around the outer edge, making the joins as neat as possible.

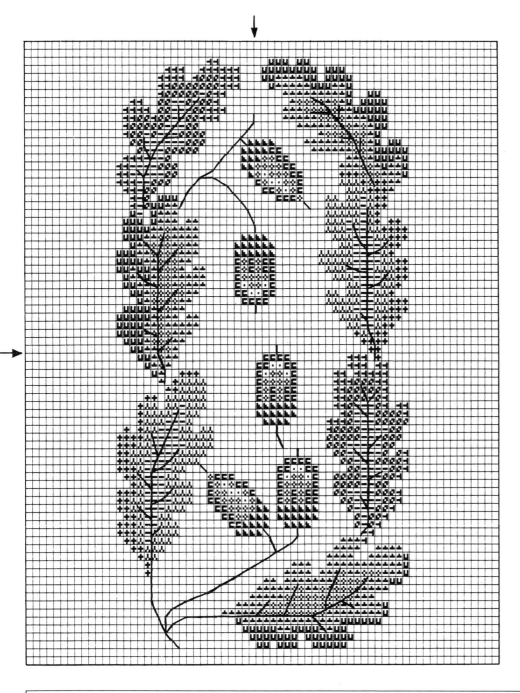

ACORN SPECTACLE CASE ▲		ANCHOR	DMC	MADEIRA
▪	Ecru	926	Ecru	Ecru
▬	Pale green	265	3348	1409
⅄	Mid-green	266	3347	1408
✚	Dark green	817	3346	1407
◄	Fawn	890	729	2209
◗	Yellowish brown	891	676	2208

		ANCHOR	DMC	MADEIRA
	Greenish brown*	889	610	2105
✦	Light brown	362	437	2012
⬢	Light rusty brown	365	435	2010
U	Rusty brown	371	433	2008
ᗡ	Brown	375	420	2104
∟	Purplish brown	379	840	1912

Note: *greenish brown* is used exclusively for the backstitching.*

· MUSHROOM STUDIES ·

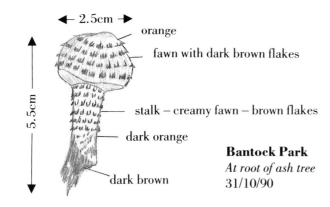

← 2.5cm →

orange

fawn with dark brown flakes

5.5cm

stalk – creamy fawn – brown flakes

dark orange

Bantock Park
At root of ash tree
31/10/90

dark brown

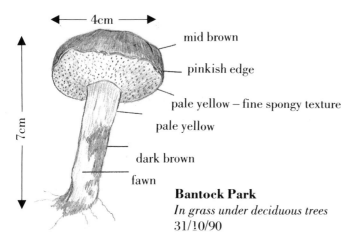

← 4cm →

mid brown

pinkish edge

7cm

pale yellow – fine spongy texture

pale yellow

dark brown

fawn

Bantock Park
In grass under deciduous trees
31/10/90

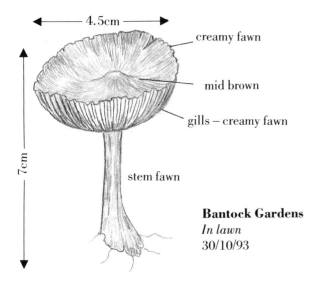

← 4.5cm →

creamy fawn

mid brown

gills – creamy fawn

7cm

stem fawn

Bantock Gardens
In lawn
30/10/93

An autumn walk in the countryside or local park almost always results in the discovery of mushrooms – sometimes common, sometimes more unusual specimens; sometimes colourful, more often brown or cream, but always fascinating. They appear overnight and change from tight knobs to full blown, mushroom-shaped fruiting bodies in a few hours. Their various colours and forms make them a delight to the embroidery designer, but they also present a problem – they are highly ephemeral.

When I am out walking, I do not always carry a camera, but I usually have a polythene bag in my pocket. When I find a mushroom that I think would be attractive in a design, I collect a sample and carry it home carefully in a bag to avoid damaging it. As soon as I arrive home, I sit down with pencil and paper and make a careful drawing of it, recording as much detail as possible, and including the exact location in which I found it, environmental details and the date.

It is important to remember that many mushrooms are very poisonous, and care should be taken when handling them, and with disposing of the specimens when your work is completed, especially if there are young children around.

Again, if you are experimenting with sketches of this type for the first time, do not be deterred by doubts as to your artistic ability – these drawings are simply for your personal use; just draw the basic shape and proportions of each find as accurately as possible, and include any interesting details. Your drawing skills will soon improve with practice.

If I can identify the mushroom from my field guide, then that is an added bonus. My drawings help me to introduce the mushrooms into my designs and my field notes help me to set them in a realistic environment. Identification helps me to extend the theme further by introducing drawings of the same species at various stages of its development, using my field guide. My field sketches become part of a composite motif – and then finally a watercolour of the finished design.

Cushion design

For my cushion I chose to design four composite motifs, each one a study of a different species of mushroom. I selected the mushrooms to give a variety of colour and form, choosing species which grew in oak and beech woodland, so that I could incorporate the designs developed in the first part of this chapter. I arranged full-sized outline drawings, with just basic shading on them, on the square which was to become the basis of my cushion pattern. Since this was to be a square cushion, I chose a small single motif from my field sketches, and repeated it in each corner. The size of my complete full-scale drawing was 45cm (18in) square. This would produce a pattern which, when worked on 14-count fabric, would cover an area 32.5cm (13in) square. The size of the cushion could be adjusted by increasing or decreasing the width of the border of plain fabric around the edge. Thus the pencil-drawn plan and individual watercolour studies were the basis of the finished design.

I placed a large sheet of graph tracing paper (10 squares to 2.5cm/1in) over the whole full-sized pencil sketch and, using the same method as for the leaves and for the autumn nuts, I traced the outline shape of the mushrooms and leaves, following the vertical and horizontal lines of the grid. Then I divided the area within each main shape into sections according to colour, trying to generalize the natural gradations. When I had a satisfactory design on

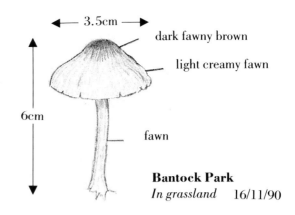

3.5cm

dark fawny brown

light creamy fawn

6cm

fawn

Bantock Park
In grassland   16/11/90

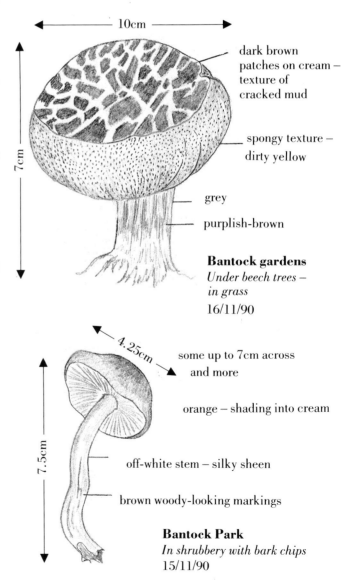

10cm

dark brown patches on cream – texture of cracked mud

spongy texture – dirty yellow

7cm

grey

purplish-brown

Bantock gardens
Under beech trees – in grass
16/11/90

4.25cm

some up to 7cm across and more

orange – shading into cream

7.5cm

off-white stem – silky sheen

brown woody-looking markings

Bantock Park
In shrubbery with bark chips
15/11/90

the graph tracing paper, I transferred the pattern to ordinary graph paper and added the essential backstitch for leaf stalks and veins.

Selecting colours

Choosing natural colours is always, I feel, the most difficult part of the exercise. When producing a design like this, not only do the colours in the individual motifs have to be appropriate, and blend well, but all the motifs together should create a pleasing overall effect. Since colour is so important a part of my creations, I always stitch all my completed designs myself, before they are launched in public. Colours that look good on the drawing board, or even placed side by side in the skeins, often look very different when they are stitched together in a design. Sometimes I try several colours for the same few stitches before I am satisfied that the effect is what I want. Colours that appear to be a perfect match, when placed by the side of a subject, can look harsh when stitched into the design. In other instances, colours that appear rather vivid when first stitched are softened when adjacent areas are embroidered with a softer blending colour. It all comes down to experiment, trial and error – and lots of patience!

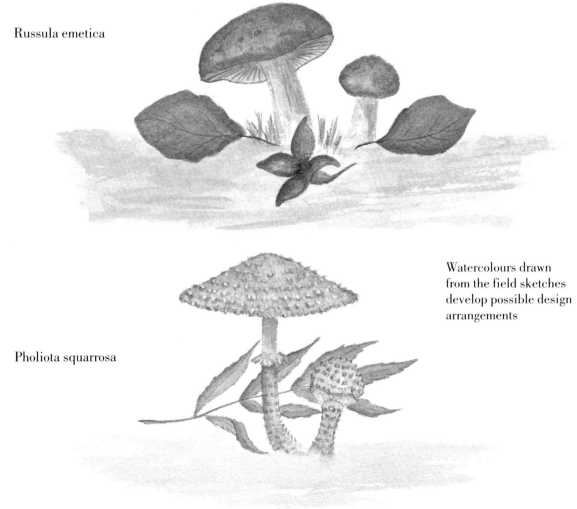

Russula emetica

Pholiota squarrosa

Watercolours drawn from the field sketches develop possible design arrangements

A pencil sketch of the full cushion design includes four composite
motifs and a small single motif, which is repeated at each corner.
This pencil sketch has been reduced in size – the original measures
45cm (18in) square. The individual composite motifs on the
full-size drawing each measure approximately 15cm × 10cm (6in × 4in).

· MUSHROOM CUSHION COVER ·

The finished cover measures 45.5cm
(18in) square.

———

· Y O U   W I L L   N E E D ·
50cm (20in) square of 14-count cream
Aida fabric • 50cm (20in) square of
matching furnishing fabric, for backing •
Two 50cm (20in) squares of strong
unbleached cotton fabric, for the inner
cover • Six-stranded embroidery
cottons, as listed in the panel on pages
36 and 37 • Cushion filler of your own
choice, or a 45.5cm (18in) square cushion
pad • 3m (3½yds) of mushroom-coloured
cord, 5mm (¼in) in diameter

Making the cover

When you have completed the embroidery,
take the two squares of unbleached cotton
fabric and, with right sides together and
taking a 2.5cm (1in) seam allowance,
machine stitch around the edges, leaving a
25cm (10in) opening at one side. Trim across
the corners and turn right side out. Insert the
filling or pad and slipstitch the opening.

Place the embroidered fabric and backing
with right sides together and repeat as for the
inner cover

To complete the cover, trim the edges with
the cord, forming it into loops at the corners
and slipstitching it in place.

Below: Stropharia aeruginosa

MUSHROOM CUSHION COVER ▲			
	ANCHOR	DMC	MADEIRA
• Ecru	926	ecru	ecru
↘ Dusky pink	893	224	0813
✖ Dark dusky pink	882	407	2310
✓ Brownish pink	914	3064	2312
Y Light red	10	351	0214
✚ Red	11	350	0213
U Deep red	13	347	0407
✦ Pale gold	362	437	2012
▫ Pale orange	363	402	2307
▸ Light orange	323	722	0307

		ANCHOR	DMC	MADEIRA
⌐	Orange	326	720	0309
↗	Pale blue green	213	504	1701
⌐	Pale green	875	503	1702
⊏	Dark blue green	876	502	1703
┼	Green	817	3346	1407
┫	Olive green	844	3012	1606
┏	Dark olive	845	3011	1607
—	Oatmeal	885	739	2014
ı	Light fawn	942	738	2013
⋀	Fawn	372	422	2102
⊐	Light brown	420	375	2104
⊱	Light golden brown	307	783	2211

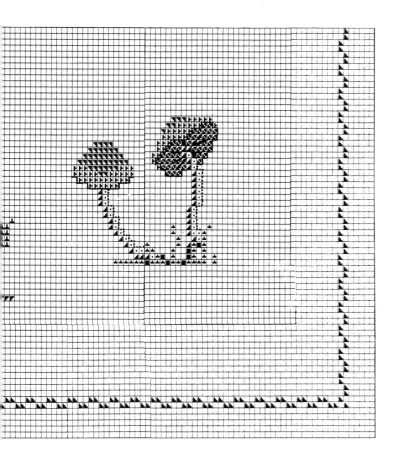

⌐	Golden brown	308	782	2212
⊥	Brown	309	780	2214
⛏	Yellowish brown	901	680	2212
	Greenish brown*	889	610	2105
T	Mid-brown	365	435	2010
Π	Rusty brown	371	433	2008
■	Dark brown	359	898	2007
⌐	Pale grey	398	415	1803
L	Purplish grey	379	840	1912

Backstitching

Greenish brown is used for backstitch only.*

Backstitch as follows: corner (repeat) mushrooms – stems in pale grey, gills and cap outline in greenish brown; top centre mushrooms – leaf stalks, collar and small mushroom cap in greenish brown; centre left mushrooms – outline mushroom cap in ecru, small mushroom stem in blue green and gills, leaf veins, twigs, and acorn in greenish brown; bottom centre mushrooms – stem and cap in fawn; beech seed stalk in rusty brown, and leaf stalks and veins in greenish brown, and centre left mushrooms – leaf stalks and veins in greenish brown, and mushroom stem in purplish grey.

AUTUMN
BERRIES

Choosing the right material for a particular purpose, and creating designs to fit into a given size of frame or aperture, are problems that present themselves to the designer as each new project is contemplated. For this section, I have created a design incorporating a group of autumn berries and explain how, by using materials of different counts, this can be enlarged or reduced to fit a variety of ready-made products.

· AIDA AND EVENWEAVE FABRICS ·

Cross stitch embroidery is best done either on Aida or on other evenweave fabrics.

Aida

Aida fabrics have a squared structure; the weft and warp threads are bunched to form blocks of regular size, with distinct needle holes at each corner, which makes them easy to count. Aida fabric is available in various 'counts'. The count is the number of holes per 2.5cm (1in), and in some cross stitch patterns the term HPI (holes per inch) is used instead of count.

Aida fabric is available in 6-count, which allows only six stitches to 2.5cm (1in), for example *Binca* or *Herta*, which is specially suitable for children, for people just starting cross stitch, for those with poor eyesight, and for teachers' demonstration pieces. At the other end of the scale, 18-count Aida, known as *Ainring*, is a fine fabric, ideal for cross stitch designs in which detail and subtle shading are employed. Between these two extremes, a wide range of counts – 7, 8, 11 and 14, for example – is available.

Other evenweaves

Other evenweave fabrics are also eminently suitable for cross stitching, having the same number of evenly-spaced warp and weft threads to 2.5cm (1inch). They include fine *Belfast linen* (32-count) and *Dublin linen* (25-count), suitable for samplers and table linen. Cross stitchers may prefer to work over two threads of linen, which is easier on the eyes and makes the design look bolder and grow faster, but still gives a fine background to the embroidery.

The pure cotton evenweave fabric *Linda* is a 27-count material, and the 52 per cent cotton/ 48 per cent rayon evenweave fabric *Lugana* is a 25-count fabric. Both are suitable for table linen, samplers and fine clothing; again, cross stitchers may prefer to work over two threads.

The popular *Hardanger* is a pure cotton evenweave fabric originating in Norway. It is woven with a double thread, which is counted as one. Cross stitch worked on this 22-count material is very fine.

Silk gauze

If your eyesight is good and you have plenty of patience, why not try a new dimension – stitching on *silk* gauze. This is a very fine fabric, ranging from a count of 30 to a count of 72. Good light and a magnifying lens are essential for this very close work. Silk gauze can be purchased already mounted in a card frame, which keeps the gauze taut and thus makes it easier to handle. The gauze itself is stiff and the fine silk strands are very strong, so it is not as difficult to stitch as it may appear at first sight. The results can be stunning. Designs perfected on a fabric with a very high count may be reduced in size to fit in small frames and pendants. The stitches appear like tiny raised beads of colour on a transparent background. Finished pieces worked on silk can be mounted against backgrounds coloured to suit the design.

Threads

When using six-stranded embroidery cotton on 22-count material or finer, you are recommended to embroider with only one strand of cotton. On 18-count fabric, two strands give a pleasing result, and on 14-count I prefer to use three strands. On coarser fabrics you need to use more strands. In any case, it is best to experiment. There are no hard and fast rules, and in the end it is the effect you wish to achieve that matters most. I like a solid effect,

covering the threads I am working over, and giving a slightly raised finish when pressed. If you want a more open finish, where the shape of each cross can be distinguished, then use fewer strands than generally recommended.

Aida and other evenweave fabrics come in a variety of colours, and there are a number of different embroidery threads now on the market, but these will be considered in later chapters of this book.

· DESIGNING TO SCALE ·

If you have an attractive square or rectangular frame, and you wish to create a design to fit into it, this can easily be done with the aid of the following simple formula.

1 First choose the count on which you wish to work (see the preceding page). For small frames, it is best to use a high count, since you can get more detail into a small space. For a larger frame, you may wish to use a fabric with a count of 14 or less (unless you intend to cover two threads per stitch).

2 Next, you need to calculate how many squares/stitches you have at your disposal on the count of your choice. Since the count of a fabric is expressed in inches, you need to convert any metric measurements to inches, so that both statistics (count and frame measurement) are in the same denomination.

Suppose your aperture is 15cm × 10cm (6in × 4in), and you have decided upon a 27-count evenweave, you then multiply the number of inches by the count:

$$6(\text{in}) \times 27 \,(\text{count}) = 162 \text{ stitches vertically}$$
$$4(\text{in}) \times 27 \,(\text{count}) = 108 \text{ stitches across}$$

3 Cut or mark out your graph paper so that you have 162 squares vertically, and 108 squares across.

Using graph paper with 10 squares to 2.5cm (1in) the area will look very large, but it gives enough space to write in clear symbols and, when worked on 27-count fabric, the design will be reduced to fit 15cm × 10cm (6in × 4in). You must also, however, remember to allow for a margin, unless you want your design to come right up to the edge of the frame.

4 The following chart shows the number of squares/stitches available to you when designing for a 15cm × 10cm (6in × 4in) frame on other counts. The lower the count, the smaller the number of stitches available to you.

	LOW		COUNT			HIGH
Count	**6**	**11**	**14**	**18**	**22**	**27**
Measurement vertically- 15cm (6in)	36	66	84	108	132	162
Measurement horizontally 10cm (4in)	24	44	56	72	88	108

Working area

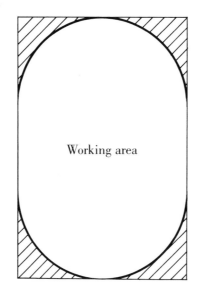

Working area

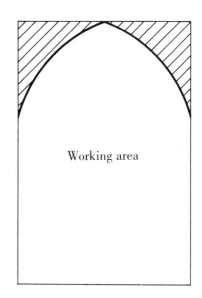

Working area

Designing for a round or oval frame

Supposing that your frame or aperture is round or oval rather than rectangular or square, you should follow the same basic procedure, but make allowances for the shaping, as described below

1 Measure the maximum length and maximum width of the aperture.

2 Follow the procedure as described for a rectangular frame.

3 Sketch in on your graph paper the shape of the aperture. To make sure that your lines are symmetrical and smooth, you may find compasses useful for a circular aperture or an artists' flexible ruler for irregular curves.

4 Blank out on your graph paper those areas which are not to be used when designing.

Calculating the size on different fabrics

If you have a favourite design already worked out on graph paper, and you want to know how large it will be if stitched on fabrics of varying counts, the calculation is very straightforward.

Taking as an example the Berries design shown overleaf, which has a maximum of 64 stitches/squares vertically and of 46 stitches/squares horizontally, divide the number of stitches by the count of the material. This will give you the dimensions in inches, which can then be converted to metric measurements.

Again, you will usually need to add a margin around these measurements.

COUNT

Number of stitches	6	11	14	18	22	27
64	10¾in 27cm	5¾in 14.75cm	4½in 11.5cm	3½in 9cm	3in 7.5cm	2½in 6.2cm
46	7½in 19.25cm	4¼in 10.5cm	3¼in 8.5cm	2½in 6.5cm	2in 5.3cm	1¾in 4.25cm

· BERRIES ·

This design comprises four types of berry, all to be found on garden shrubs throughout the autumn months – rose hips, pyracanthus berries, snowberries and tiny crab apples. I gathered these in November, and arranged them in a little bouquet together with some variegated ivy. Then I made pencil drawings of the group, in the same way as I did for the mushrooms. Berries last longer than mushrooms, however, and once I had worked out the outline shapes for the design on graph paper, I was able to choose the colours by directly matching berries with cottons. The berries sat in front of me, in a glass jar, as I designed and stitched the samples. This enabled me to make adjustments to the colours I had chosen initially, and also to make refinements to shading, and the shapes of berries and leaves.

I stitched the pattern first on an 18-count fabric, as this is a good scale to work on – small enough to show off the design to its best advantage, but large enough to enable one to unpick and alter colours without too much difficulty. I then stitched the same design on 14-count and 22-count fabrics, and on 40-count silk gauze.

Assembling
14-count sample
This is mounted in an oval frame 17.5cm × 12.5cm (7in × 5in). The worked design is laced over an oval card, which fits snugly into the back of the frame. The backing plate is then replaced.

18-count sample
This sample is displayed in a greetings card measuring 20cm × 15cm (8in × 6in) with an oval aperture 14cm × 9.5cm (5½in × ¾in), following the mounting instructions shown on the card.

22-count sample
This sample is mounted in a glass paperweight, 10cm × 7cm (4in × 2¾in), following the manufacturer's mounting instructions.

40-count sample
The silk gauze is left in its card frame, and mounted in a 12.5cm (5in) square frame.

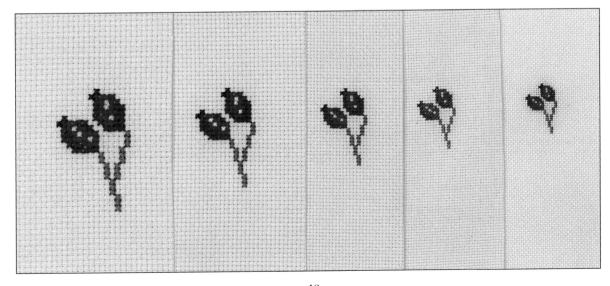

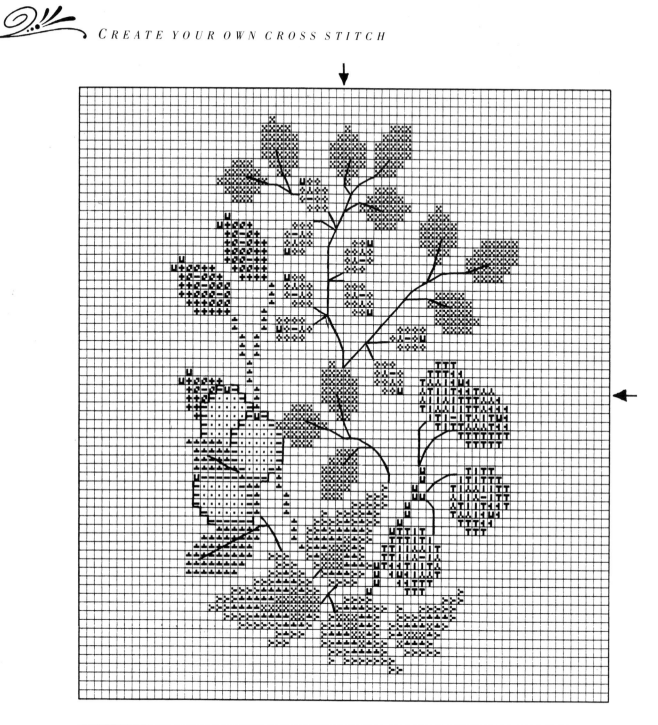

BERRIES ▲	ANCHOR	DMC	MADEIRA
· White	1	Blanc	White
⅄ Deep pink	10	351	0214
◰ Bright red	335	606	0209
❖ Red	13	349	0212
✛ Dark red	799	816	0511
I Yellow	295	726	0109
T Deep yellow	298	725	0108
⊱ Pale green	265	3348	1409
♣ Green	817	3346	1407
✕ Dark green	268	3345	1406
⊟ Pale fawn	387	822	1908
⊢ Light brown	375	420	2104
U Dark brown	905	3031	2003

Backstitching

Backstitch all stalks except for those of the snowberry and ivy in dark brown; snowberry outlines, stalks and leaf veins, and ivy stalks in dark green, and pyracanthus leaf veins in pale green.

GARDEN FLOWERS

One of my favourite subjects for embroidery, designing flowers from life, can prove a challenge. This chapter looks at the ways of achieving a pleasing design from this complex subject. Also discussed are the different types of coloured background available to enhance your design, and the merits of Flower Threads.

· SEASONAL AVAILABILITY OF FLOWERS ·

Flowers are surely the most popular subjects for embroidery, and have been throughout the history of this art. Roses, cornflowers, pinks and poppies appear in some of the oldest samplers, and in modern pattern books flowers still remain firm favourites.

When designing directly from nature, however, flowers present a problem. Each species has its own season for flowering, and sometimes these periods are very short. Even in the tropics, where flowers may be available all the year, particular species flower only in certain months.

If you are going to specialize in creating flower patterns, it is essential that you assemble a good record of your own favourite flowers, one to which you can refer at any time of the year. I use three kinds of record – pressed specimens, sketches and watercolours, and photographs. Each has its advantages and its disadvantages, and each helps to complement the information afforded by the other two.

Pressed specimens

This method is ideal for preserving leaves (see pages 10–21). All deciduous leaves press satisfactorily, and leaves from flowering plants are useful for inclusion in designs. Where appropriate, I like to include some leaves with the flowers in my designs, but there are limitations: in nature few leaves appear in perfect outline; some are curled, or appear end on, and too many flat specimens will make an embroidery design look unnatural.

Flowers, too, can be pressed, but I find few of these satisfactory. They often look faded, and of course lose their shape and form. Pansies and other flowers that have flat surfaces may press adequately, but pressed specimens of cup-bell-shaped and tubular flowers are of little use.

Sketches and watercolours

This is probably the ideal method, because you can sketch the flowers in the exact position you choose, and superfluous background, which confuses the image, can be left out. To use this method, however, you have to be able to draw with reasonable accuracy, and you must have the time to sit down quietly and concentrate on getting a good likeness. Painting the flower provides an invaluable record of colour and shading for your reference bank, but it may take several hours to complete a small group of flowers to your satisfaction. When I have time, this is the method of recording information that I prefer – but for most of us time is at a premium.

Photographs

The miracle of modern photography enables you to capture a flower on film in a matter of seconds. Good quality colour film provides as accurate a record of colour as you could hope to achieve. I use a 35mm single-lens-reflex camera, with a telephoto attachment. The telephoto lens enables me to get very close to the flower, recording all the detail precisely. It also helps me to compose my shot more easily than with the standard lens. Having said this, however, even the simplest camera will give an adequate result for your purposes, providing you get as close to the subject as the camera allows, and adjust the focus perfectly.

EMBROIDERY FABRICS IN VARIOUS
· COLOURS ·

The majority of cross stitch patterns are designed to be embroidered on either cream or white material, and these are the two colours most widely available. There is, however, a wide range of colours on the market if you take the trouble to seek them out, and I think that it is a great pity that they are not used more often. The brighter greens and reds are often embroidered with Christmas motifs, but there is a good choice of softer shades available for more delicate designs. A pale blue may be chosen to suggest background sky, for example, or a pale green might be used for a watery scene with just a little backstitching for details.

The bellpull (see overleaf) was worked on eau-de-nil because I felt that this pale green was the perfect foil for the vivid colours of the flowers. For the primula design (see page 56), I chose the very palest shade of pink, to reflect the deeper pinks in the flowers. I embroidered the pansy design on 'pewter' because the pale blue-grey complemented the darker colours in the design itself.

The firescreen presented more of a problem, because the design included a wide spectrum of colours – reds, yellows and white, blues and mauves, greens and browns. It also included a variety of types of flower, from the diminutive white and pale green snowdrop to the vivid anemones, and the reds and greens of holly and honeysuckle berries. To find a colour that helped to enhance the paler flowers, while not diminishing the colours of the brighter flowers and berries, was a difficult task. It also had to be a colour which would look well with the reddish brown of the firescreen frame. Eventually, I settled for parchment.

The choice of colour is a very personal thing, and everyone has his or her own preferences. All I would urge you to do is to experiment with a range of coloured backgrounds when you are designing. If you cannot obtain a good supply of coloured fabrics at your local needlework shop, try mail order (see page 128).

Flower Threads

The original Flower Threads come from Denmark, where they are produced for the Danish Handcraft Guild, which is dedicated to the promotion of a wide range of needlecrafts. The original Danish Flower Thread was introduced in 1929 by Else Johnson, who first embroidered a table cloth with this unique thread. It is a matte, pure cotton thread, twisted into a single soft strand and dyed in a range of 100 subtle shades. The colour scale that was used for the original Danish Flower Threads was based largely on the exquisite flower designs produced by Gerda Bengtsson and from the colours in traditional Danish embroidery.

DMC have now produced a similar Flower Thread. It is made of pure Californian combed cotton and has a matte finish. It is twisted into a single soft strand and it is available in 20m (21¾yds) skeins in a range of 180 colourful shades. The natural colours and softness of Flower Threads make them ideal for embroidery on cotton or linen.

Since the individual strands of Flower Thread are thicker than a single strand of stranded cotton, only one strand is required to work with on 18-count and finer fabrics. On 14-count, either one or two strands can be used, depending on the effect you want to achieve. On more open fabrics, two strands should be used.

· BELLPULL ·

For the bellpull project, I chose fuchsias as my subject. They have always been one of my favourite flowers, and their pendulous, lantern-shaped heads seemed to me the perfect subject for a repeat pattern. If you wish to follow this method to produce your own repeat pattern, similarly suitable subjects might be wisteria or clematis.

———

· YOU WILL NEED ·
To make a pattern by this method:
Photographs and other reference material of your chosen flower • Drawing materials and graph papers (see page 12)

For the fuchsia bellpull, finished size 17.5cm × 51cm (7in × 20in):
30.5 × 61cm (12in × 24in) of 18-count eau-de-nil Aida fabric • 23cm × 57cm (9in × 22½in) of silk lining fabric • 17.5cm × 51cm (7in × 20in) of iron-on interfacing • Flower Threads, as listed in the panel on page 54 • A pair of wooden bellpull hangers, 17.5cm (7in) across (for suppliers, see page 128)

1 I drew the fuchsias first from some of my own photographs, but the most detailed ones that I had were of pink and red blooms, and I visualized something more flamboyant for my bellpull. Looking through gardening magazines, I found some pictures of fuchsias in the exact shades I wanted. The photographs were small

and the detail not very distinct, but I found that I could marry the detail from my own photographs with the colours from the magazine, and in this way the fuchsias evolved.

2 The finished size of the bellpull was to be 17.5cm (7in) across by 51cm (20in) down, and I wanted to repeat the design three times. I wanted a 2cm (¾in) margin, extending down each side. The design had to be no more than 14cm (5½in) across; when worked on 18-count material, this would allow me 99 squares/ stitches across to work with. I also calculated that I could use about the same number of

squares/stitches lengthwise. In fact, the finished design was 97 squares across by 90 squares down – well within these parameters.

3 My drawing needed to be enlarged to double the size. I could have taken it to the photocopiers, but decided to enlarge it by the traditional method of covering the drawing with a grid; drawing a grid of squares twice the size on a separate piece of paper, and then copying the drawing square by square to the larger grid.

4 I covered the new enlarged drawing with a sheet of graph tracing paper, with 10 squares to 2.5cm (1in), and marked out the main lines of the flowers and leaves, following the horizontal and vertical lines of the grid.

5 When planning a repeat design, you should not have straight lines across the work where one section ends and the next one begins. The bottom of the design should interlock with the top of the same design when it is repeated below. In a very densely-stitched design, you can plan the join so that it is very difficult to see where the first pattern ends and the repeat begins. In my open fuchsia design, the line is not so easily disguised, but by making the upper leaf project into the space to the left of the half-open flower, the straight line has been avoided and the repeat sections interlock.

6 To give the fuchsias a three-dimensional quality, care had to be exercized in the choice of colours. You usually need three shades of the same colour to differentiate between areas in deep shade, semi-shade and full sunlight. If you examine the key to the pattern you will see that this is what I have tried to do.

Making the fuchsia bellpull
Embroider the design, using one strand of Flower Thread throughout, then trim the Aida fabric to measure 23cm × 58cm (9in × 23in).

Centre the iron-on interfacing on the back of the design and iron in place.

Make a 12mm (½in) turning down each long side of the Aida and press. Turn and press the long edges of the lining fabric, making sure it is just slightly narrower than the Aida strip, so that it will not be visible on the right side. Hem one long edge of the lining to the back of the Aida, just within the edge, and repeat on the opposite side.

Turn under the top and bottom edges by 6mm (¼in) and 3cm (1¼in) and hem, stitching by hand to make slots for the hanger rods. Press carefully on the wrong side, and insert the rods.

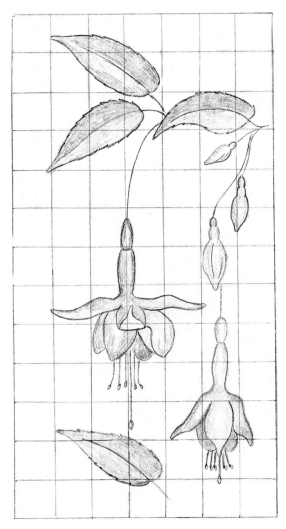

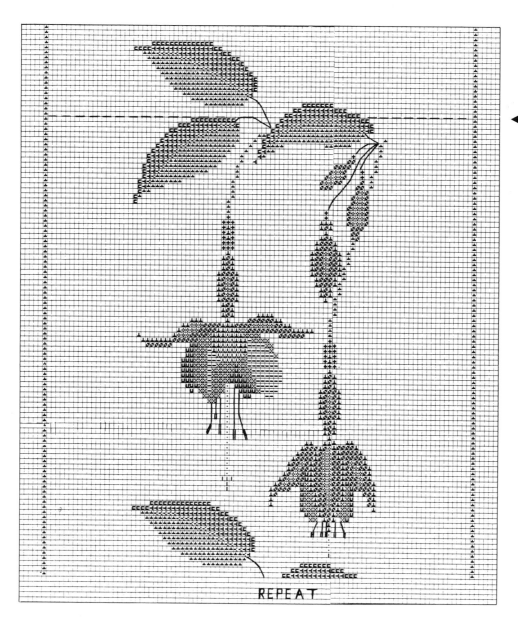

◄ Continue second
and third pattern
from this line

REPEAT

FUCHSIAS ▲	DMC (Flower threads)	DANISH (Flower threads)
• Pale pink	2776	69
I Pink	2760	12
⅄ Deep pink	2309	86
Darker pink*	2899	12
❖ Bright red	2666	97
⌀ Deep red	2304	400
— Mauve	2209	233
✕ Light purple	2532	234
⊔ Purple	2394	5
⊥ Light maroon	2815	411

	DMC	DANISH
✚ Maroon	2902	4
⊰ Pale green	2369	99
⊥ Mid-green	2320	9
⊣ Green	2319	238
⊏ Dark green	2890	210

Backstitching

Darker pink* is used for backstitching only. Use mid-green for leaf and bud stalks, pale pink for stamens, and darker pink for the tips of the stamens.

= Darker pink

——— All other backstitching

· POT POURRI COVERS ·

For this pair of pot pourri covers,
I chose pansies and primulas as my
subjects. These popular and brightly-
coloured flowers are in bloom for a good
part of the year, and can be grown in
window boxes and patio planters as
well as in garden borders.
The designs were developed from
watercolours (see below).

· Y O U   W I L L   N E E D ·
*For each cover, with a finished size of
19cm (7½in) diameter, including a lace
edging, 12mm (½in) deep:*

20cm (8in) square of 14-count Aida
fabric, in a colour of your choice •
Flower Threads, as listed in the
appropriate panel • 70cm (¾yd) of lace,
12mm (½in) wide, for trimming • 1m
(1yd) of ribbon, 6mm (¼in) wide, in a
colour of your choice, for trimming •
Pot pourri and a jar, with a top 7.5cm
(3in) in diameter

Making the covers

Both covers are made in the same way.
Complete the embroidery, using two strands of
Flower Thread. Take a pair of compasses and
place the point in the exact centre of the design.
Mark out a circle with a radius of 8cm (3¼in).
If you have no compasses, you can use a
suitable plate, but it is difficult to centre the
design with this method.

Carefully cut out your circle of material and
overlock the edges with machine stitching.
Join the short edges of the lace together with a
tiny french seam and hand-stitch the lace
around the edge, frilling it slightly.

Fill your jar with pot pourri and place the
cover over the top. Secure with the ribbon,
making a neat bow to give an attractive finish.

The designs were first
painted in watercolours
before being transferred to
graph paper and
converted into chart form.

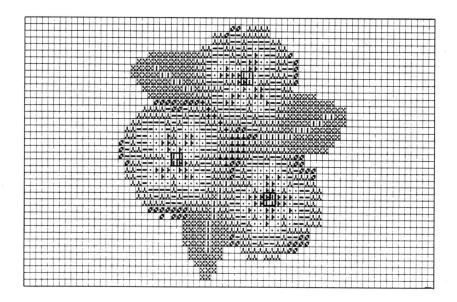

PRIMULAS ▲		DMC (Flower threads)	DANISH (Flower threads)
▪	White	Blanc	600
▬	Pale pink	2818	1
⋏	Pink	2309	86
◰	Dark pink	2326	88
✚	Dark red	2814	205
⊩	Yellow	2726	46
▮	Pale green	2471	40
✕	Green	2469	10
⊥	Dark green	2937	237

Backstitching
Flower centres are backstitched in green.

PANSIES ▼		DMC (Flower threads)	DANISH (Flower threads)
▪	White	Blanc	600
◳	Yellow	2726	46
▬	Pale mauve	2210	232
⋏	Mauve	2209	233
◆	Purple	2532	234
✚	Dark purple	2531	5
⊔	Navy	2823	201
▮	Pale green	2471	40
✕	Green	2469	10
⊥	Dark green	2937	237
■	Black	2310	240

Backstitching *Flower centres are backstitched in black.*

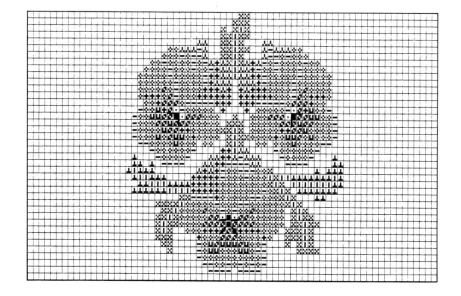

· FIRESCREEN ·

· YOU WILL NEED ·

For a firescreen measuring
71cm × 49.5cm (28in × 19½in), with an
aperture measuring 40.5cm × 45.5cm
(16in × 18in):

66cm × 68.5cm (26in × 27in) of 14-
count parchment Aida fabric • Flower
Threads, as listed in the panel on pages
60, 62, 64 and 65 • Firescreen (for
suppliers, see page 128)

For the firescreen project I opted for a bold design, incorporating flowers from the four seasons. The design would be embroidered on 14-count Aida, and the flowers chosen are all personal favourites, selected for this reason and also because, when seen together, the effect is both colourful and pleasing.

If you wish to make your own design, you might like to use the simple border shown here, incorporating your own flowers within the design panels. Following the method described for the mushroom design, starting on page 28, you could first draw and then paint each panel in watercolour. In this way you will be able to get a fairly accurate idea of what the finished panel will look like before you start stitching.

1 I began the design by taking a piece of 14-count Aida, measuring 66cm × 68.5cm (26in × 27in). The firescreen aperture measures 40.5cm × 45.5cm (16in × 18in), which would provide a working area of 224 squares across and 252 squares down. I counted out the squares on my piece of Aida and basted around the exact area, using a light-coloured sewing thread.

2 It is important that the actual embroidered area does not run right up to the wood surround, so I basted a second line, 12 squares in from the outer boundary. This demarcated the stitching area.

If you are contemplating designing a symmetrical border, similar to the one shown here, you may find it easier if you have an odd number of squares, across and down, so that your central point is a square rather than the intersection of lines between squares. In the case of this particular screen, this would entail moving your basting line in by one square on one side and at either the top or bottom.

3 The design for each section was made following the method used for the cushion cover (see pages 28–35).

Finishing the screen
The firescreen embroidery has been divided into four charts, the pictures on page 63 showing the order in which they are arranged. The chart for Spring is on page 60; Summer is on page 62; Autumn is on page 64, and Winter is on page 65. Start by basting central horizontal and vertical lines on the fabric to mark the divisions between the seasons, then complete each season as a separate picture, until you have finished all four, including the border.

When you have completed the embroidery, using two strands of Flower Thread throughout, steam-press it carefully on the wrong side.

Stretch the finished embroidery over the mounting board provided with the firescreen. Lace the edges together across the back with strong thread before inserting the embroidery into the firescreen and securing it in place.

SPRING ▲	DMC (Flower threads)	DANISH (Flower threads)				
• Ecru	Ecru	0	**L** Mustard	2725	203
Pale Pink*	2818	1	**Y** Yellowish green	2734	218
⅄ Pink	2776	69	**T** Dark yellowish green	2732	26
Π Cyclamen pink	2916	234	**I** Pale green	2369	99
— Dusky pink	2223	3	**⅃** Green	2469	10
❖ Dark dusky pink	2222	235	**🖸** Light blue green	2320	9
⁄ Purplish pink	2608	232	**✕** Blue green	2319	238
⊣ Deep purplish pink	2719	37	**+** Dark green	2937	237
↘ Dull mauve	2315	11	**⊦** Brown	2840	216
Red*	2666	99			
🖸 Dull red	2570	205			
⊣ Dark red	2814	205			
⊑ Maroon	2902	4			
⌐ Yellow	2726	46			

Backstitching

Red* and pale pink* are used for backstitching only. Use ecru for the centres of the lenten roses, light blue green for the cyclamen flower and leaf stalks, pale green for the leaf veins, brown for the hazel twig, red for the female flowers on the hazel twig and pale pink for the cyclamen flower centre.

SUMMER ▲	DMC (Flower threads)	DANISH (Flower threads)
• White	Blanc	600
━ Ecru	Ecru	0
⅄ Pale pink	2818	1
⌁ Deep pink	2899	2
⊦ Purplish pink	2719	37
I Mauve	2210	232
⊣ Deep mauve	2532	234
⊏ Purple	2531	5
⊡ Red	2666	97
T Dark red	2815	411
⌊ Maroon	2902	4

❖ Light green	2472	223
❧ Mid-green	2471	40
⅃ Green	2469	10
⅁ Yellowish green	2732	26
⊔ Bottle green	2890	210
✛ Dark green	2937	237
■ Black	2310	240

Backstitching

*Ecru is used for the anemone centres, light green to outline the
clematis flowers, purplish pink for the tip of the clematis bud,
two strands of dark green for the clematis stems and tendrils,
and dark brown for the clematis centres.*

SPRING

SUMMER

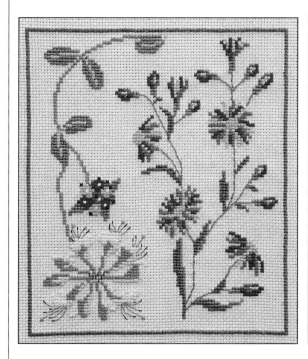

AUTUMN

WINTER

AUTUMN ▲		DMC (Flower threads)	DANISH (Flower threads)
•	White	Blanc	600
−	Pink	2776	69
❖	Dusky pink	2761	12
◤	Deep pink	2899	2
◲	Red	2666	97
◣	Deep red	2815	411
I	Mauve	2210	232
⊣	Dark mauve	2532	234
⊐	Purple	2394	5
⅄	Yellow	2727	16
✕	Mustard	2725	203

⊦	Deep yellow	2726	46
◥	Orange	2740	53
T	Deep orange	2946	504
➤	Yellowish green	2734	218
◳	Dark yellowish green	2732	26
⊥	Green	2469	10
+	Dark green	2937	237
⊔	Dark brown	2938	216

Backstitching

Use one strand of dark yellowish green for the honeysuckle stamens, and one of dark brown for the honeysuckle centre and ends of stamens, and two strands of green for the Michaelmas daisy stems.

WINTER ▲		DMC (Flower threads)	DANISH (Flower threads)
·	White	Blanc	600
◘	Red	2666	97
┗	Dark red	2815	411
⅄	Pale yellow	2727	16
┣	Yellow	2726	46
✕	Mustard	2725	203
	Light blue green*	2320	9
T	Blue green	2319	238
I	Very pale green	2715	302
⸜	Light green	2471	40

⊥	Bright green	2469	10
✚	Green	2937	237
⊏	Dark green	2937	210
⊣	Brown	2610	251
⊔	Dark brown	2938	216

Backstitching
Use light blue green* (used for backstitching only) for the snowdrop flowers, light green for the outline of the jasmine flowers, and brown for the holly spines and twigs, using one strand of thread in the needle in each case; use two strands of bright green for the snowdrop stalks.

PETS

Everyone has his or her favourite animal, and
a cross stitch picture can be a treasured
memento of a much-loved pet. To add interest
to a simple portrait, try setting it against a
fabric-painted background or use metallic
threads to produce subtle highlights, to give
your designs a distinctive quality.

· SPECIAL EFFECTS ·

The designs on the following pages are all intended for mounting in greetings cards, but they can just as easily be used for small pictures. All of these designs show one or more simple special effects. Some have a background tinted with fabric paint and highlighted with felt-tip pens. If you are going to colour materials that will require washing, check that the paints you use are colour fast!

Some designs incorporate blending filaments – 'Basic' shades, 'Hi lustre' and 'Glow-in-the-dark'. The effects of these cannot be fully appreciated from photographs, but I hope that you will experiment with them, because the results can be delightful. Mixtures of several colours of stranded thread can be used to produce special effects not possible when using one colour in the needle at a time.

The message here, therefore, is that you should experiment with all sorts of combinations to give your designs that distinctive touch.

Tinted backgrounds

Most cross stitch designs are created against backgrounds which are simply of one colour. Instead of working your design on plain white or cream Aida, or even on one of the pastel-coloured fabrics, why not experiment and add a fun dimension by the use of fabric paints or dyes? There are several well-known brands available, but check that they are fade- and wash-proof.

Applied simply with a watercolour paint brush (or if you are more adventurous, with an air brush) you can create a variegated or dappled background appropriate for your subject, giving the illusion of water, grass, sky, woodland, undergrowth, or whatever – and you will have the satisfaction of knowing that it is

unique! For small delicate designs, I prefer simply to tint the material. If the painting is too heavy, it detracts from the embroidery itself.

Do remember, though, to prepare the fabric before you begin to stitch your design. Paint will spread on the material, and the more watery the application of paint, the more it will spread. If you try to add to your background after you have done your stitching, you may have a disaster on your hands!

Applying colour

Choose the threads for your design, and have them handy as you mix your paints to avoid colours that do not go well together.

To apply colour with a brush, simply put a small quantity of paint onto a mixing palette or saucer and dilute with water until you have the density of colour you require. As the number of colours available is relatively limited, it is often necessary to mix them to give more subtle shades. Always test your colours on a piece of spare material before you begin.

You may prefer to apply the paint with an air brush; there are several makes and various types on the market. The choice will depend on how much you intend to use the instrument and how much you want to spend.

Before you load the reservoir of your air brush make sure that the paint is of a free-running consistency, and there are no tiny lumps in it – otherwise you will clog your instrument. Hold the air brush 10–15cm (4–6in) away from your fabric. Move your hand in a free swinging motion, and build up the colour tone gradually. For a fine line, hold the air brush tip closer to the fabric. Practise on spare fabric first.

After the application of each colour, empty the reservoir and run clear water through the air brush to remove every trace of paint. Be very careful to clean your instrument thoroughly before putting it away. A tiny bit of dried paint can block the airway and prove hard to clear.

Metallic threads

Way back in history, embroiderers in ancient Egypt and in China enriched their designs by introducing multiple fibres into their work. Later on, in the middle ages and even more recently, Europeans did the same. In those early days, embroiderers were not content to work in a single type of thread – cotton for cross stitch and wool for needlepoint – as we do today. They combined silk, linen and metallic threads with cotton and woollen fibres, giving their embroideries a strong visual appeal. In more recent centuries, this freedom of choice became more restricted, and some of the vitality, life and lustre was lost from our needlework.

For the last two decades, Kreinik have been producing metallic threads which have revolutionized the opportunities available to embroiderers. To some people, metallic threads have an instant, albeit superficial appeal, because with them they can add fun and glitz to a design and make an eye–catching statement. A growing number of needleworkers, however, are coming to appreciate the more subtle qualities of a design enhanced by metallic threads. Blending filaments have a reflective quality that creates the effect of light on water, snow and frost. They also lend a realism to scenes incorporating moonlight and starlight. Where birds, such as the kingfisher or the hummingbird, have iridescent feathers, metallic threads add a new dimension. The possibilities are endless.

In my designs, which are in general small and detailed, I use mainly the blending filaments; these are one-ply metallic threads, most often used in conjunction with stranded cotton for cross stitch. Blending filaments can be used alone, especially in work on 22-count or finer fabrics. Kreinik produce a wide range of blending filaments in 'Basic' shades and in 'Hi lustre' tones. If you prefer bolder embroideries, there is, in addition to the blending filament range, a large choice of progressively heavier threads available.

Work containing metallic threads, except Japan threads, can be machine washed and even tumble dried on a low setting. Care, however, must be exercised when ironing: never use a steam iron, and do not iron directly on the metallic thread, but always use a cloth. Work can also be dry cleaned.

Threading techniques for blending filament You should use no more than 45cm (18in) of thread at a time. Double the thread about 5cm (2in) at one end, and insert the loop through the eye of the needle. Pull the loop over the point of the needle and gently pull the loop towards the end of the eye to secure the thread to the needle. If you are using a combination of blending filament and stranded cotton, thread the latter through the eye in the usual way, and clip it to match the length of the blending filament.

Kreinik threads are available from an increasing number of needlework shops, but if you have problems see page 128 for mail-order suppliers.

· PET CAT PORTRAIT ·

1 Cats can be very appealing, but from my experience they are not easy subjects to photograph. When they are not sleeping, they are often camera-shy, and they have an aloof disregard for anyone who tries to get them to pose. The only way to get a good photograph of a cat, as with most animals (and people for that matter) is to catch them unawares.

2 The photograph of our own cat, Timmy, was rather small, so I had to begin by enlarging it. I concentrated on his head and shoulders in order to get as much detail into my design as the space would allow.

With basting stitches, I first marked out on the fabric the position, size and shape of the oval aperture, and then counted the number of squares, vertically and horizontally, that were available to me for designing. I could then ensure that the sketch from which I made my design would fit into the space comfortably, allowing for a margin.

3 Using an air brush, I sprayed the background in a light shade of blue. This colour would, I felt, be a suitable foil for the black and white fur and the yellow eyes of the cat. The dye was then fixed by ironing, following the manufacturer's instructions.

4 When the design had been completed, following the process described for the mushroom cushion (page 28), I embroidered it on the 18-count Aida, using two strands of cotton throughout, except for the eye, where a metallic blending filament was substituted for one of the cotton strands.

5 Finally, I pressed the design; ironed the interfacing to the back; trimmed the finished piece, and mounted it in the card.

TIMMY ▲		KREINIK	ANCHOR	DMC	MADEIRA
·	White		1	Blanc	White
Y	Pink		893	224	0813
—	Lemon	054F			
			288	445	0103
⊥	Light grey		398	415	0103
⌀	Grey		400	317	1714
+	Dark grey		401	413	1713
■	Black		403	310	Black

Backstitching

Use white for whiskers; black for the nose, mouth and the side of the ear, and lemon above and below the pupils.

· PET DOG PORTRAIT ·

1 Most people have a pet at some stage in their life, and not only are dogs very popular, but they are also frequently photographed. It is not always easy to get a dog to pose, but with perseverance it is possible to get a good likeness.

It is important to determine from the first whether you wish to do a portrait of the head and shoulders only, or whether you want to include the whole of the animal in your design. For a first attempt, I think it is best to concentrate on the head and shoulders. This enables you to get more detail into your design, capturing some of those characteristics that make your dog unique.

Again, for a first attempt choose a photograph with the dog's head either in profile or full face – three-quarter view portraits are notoriously difficult to get right.

The photograph from which I chose to work was one of our own dog, Gealas.

2 The procedure followed was the same as for the cat portrait: again, I started by cutting a piece of Aida fabric to the working size (20cm × 15cm/8in × 6in), and calculating the number of squares each way within the oval aperture.

3 Instead of the blue used for the cat portrait, I sprayed the background with a light shade of green, selected to set off the deep russett of the dog's coat. The dye was then fixed by ironing.

4 The design was stitched with two threads of stranded cotton throughout, and finished in the same way as the cat portrait.

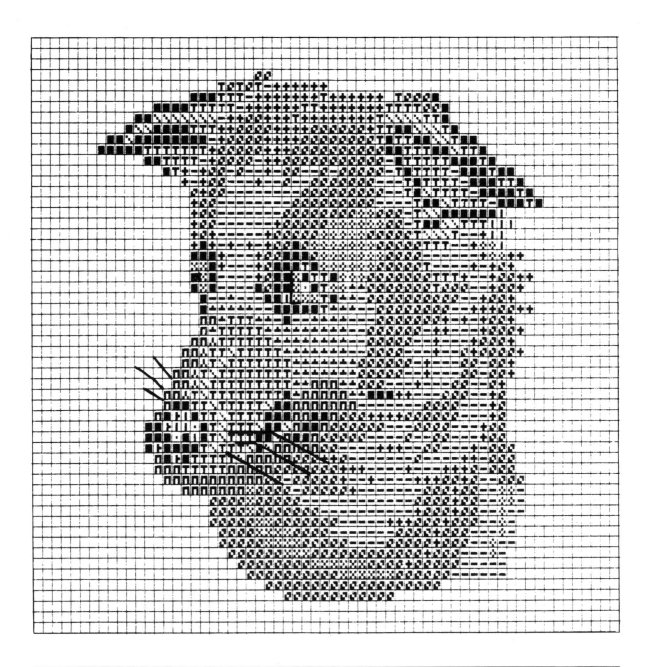

GEALAS ▲	ANCHOR	DMC	MADEIRA
▪ White	1	Blanc	White
▬ Light orange brown	363	402	2307
✤ Light golden brown	307	977	2301
◨ Golden brown	308	976	2302
✖ Yellowish brown	944	869	2105
⅄ Pinkish brown	882	407	2312
◥ Brown	936	632	2311
✚ Reddish brown	355	975	2303
T Dark brown	905	3031	2003

	ANCHOR	DMC	MADEIRA
⊓ Very dark brown	382	3371	2004
⊥ Brown flecked	308	976	2302
(one strand of each)	905	3031	2003
❙ Light grey	399	318	1802
⊦ Grey	400	317	1714
■ Black	403	310	Black

Backstitching
Backstitch the eye and eye highlight in white and the whiskers in black.

· GOLDFISH ·

> **· YOU WILL NEED ·**
> 15cm × 10cm (6in × 4in) of 18-count
> cream Aida fabric • 15cm × 10cm
> (6in × 4in) of iron-on interfacing •
> Stranded embroidery cottons and
> metallic blending filaments, in the
> colours listed in the panel • Pale
> turquoise blue fabric dye • Paint brush •
> Card measuring 15cm × 10cm
> (6in × 4in), with an circular aperture
> measuring 8cm (3¼in), for suppliers see
> page 128

1 Goldfish are very popular as children's pets, as well as being restful companions for many adults. I had no photographs of goldfish, and so had to resort to pictures in an old book. I drew in my own waterweed and background.

2 The design space available was worked out in exactly the same way as for the Cat portrait (see page 70). In this case, I chose a pale turquoise blue fabric paint for the background, applying it with light horizontal brushstrokes. Since this was to be a small delicate design, I was careful not to make the background too heavy. As for the airbrushed portraits of the Cat and Dog, the fabric dye was then fixed by ironing.

3 When the design sketches and chart had been worked out, following the method used for the mushroom cushion (see page 28), I stitched my goldfish design, centring it within the circle that I had marked on the fabric with basting stitches.

The basic colours used were stranded cottons, but two Kreinik metallic blending filaments were also incorporated into the design. The yellow metallic has flecks of orange and greeny-blue in it, combining well with the orange shades used in the goldfish. The metallic thread reflects the light, and is just perfect for the fish scales and for the shiny tail and dorsal fin. Most of the design is embroidered with one strand of cotton blended with one of metallic, but the head, back and lower fins are worked with two strands of cotton, while the highlights on the fish are stitched with two strands of yellow metallic thread only. The water is highlighted with a blue metallic thread combined with a blue stranded thread, and the waterweed is stitched with two threads of stranded cotton, contrasting with the sheen of the water.

4 The completed design was mounted in the card in the same way as the Cat (see page 70).

· RABBIT ·

> **· YOU WILL NEED ·**
> 20cm × 15cm (8in × 6in) of 18-count
> cream Aida fabric • 20cm × 15cm
> (8in × 6in) of iron-on interfacing •
> Stranded embroidery cottons, in the
> colours listed in the panel • Blue, green
> and brown fabric paints • Paint brushes •
> Green felt-tip pen • Card measuring
> 20cm × 15cm (8in × 6in), with an oval
> aperture measuring 14cm × 9.5cm
> (5½in × 3¾in), for suppliers see
> page 128

1 The design space available was worked out from the fabric in exactly the same way as for

the previous animal portraits. I was lucky enough to find a clear photograph of a rabbit which was sufficiently detailed for me to be able to trace the main outlines directly onto my squared paper. I then added my own details and background tufts of grass.

2 With blue fabric paint and using horizontal

brush strokes, I painted in the sky. This was left to dry and was then fixed by ironing before the grass was added, this time with various shades of green and brown, applied with vertical brushstrokes. Again, the paints were fixed by ironing.

3 I embroidered the rabbit with two strands of cotton in the needle throughout, centring it within the oval previously marked out with basting stitches.

4 When I had completed the design, I felt that I needed some foreground grasses. These were drawn with a few strokes from a green felt-tip pen. If the design had been intended for something that was likely to be laundered, this would obviously not have been possible, but a textile picture offers a much greater freedom of choice in this respect. It is wise, however, always to fix any dyes applied before stitching, as these might stain your cottons while you stitch.

5 The completed design was mounted in the card in the same way as the Cat (see page 70).

RABBIT ▲	ANCHOR	DMC	MADEIRA
· Ecru	926	Ecru	Ecru
— Pale pink	892	225	0814
✧ Pink	893	224	0813
◄ Pale green	265	3348	1409
⊢ Green	266	3347	1408
⅄ Fawn	887	372	2110
⬥ Pale brown	392	642	1906
◨ Brown	903	640	1905

❘ Pale grey-brown	830	644	1907
✚ Mid-grey	8581	646	1812
Grey*	401	413	1713
■ Black	403	310	Black

Backstitching
Grey* is used only for backstitching the whiskers; the eye highlight is in ecru; all other backstitching is in black.

...... Whiskers
——— Other backstitching

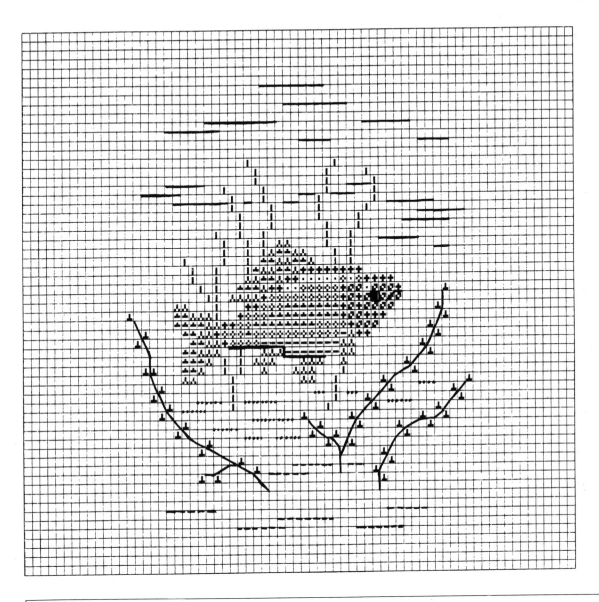

GOLDFISH ▲	KREINIK	ANCHOR	DMC	MADEIRA
White*		1	Blanc	White
• Yellow metallic	091			
▬ Deep yellow		303	742	0114
♠ Light orange		304	741	0201
♠ Light orange metallic	{091			
(one strand of each)		304	741	0201
♦ Orange		316	970	0204
♣ Orange metallic	{091			
(one strand of each)		316	970	0204
✚ Brownish orange		324	922	0310
Pale blue metallic*	{014			
(one strand of each)		849	927	1708
Blue metallic*	{014			
(one strand of each)		850	926	1707

Ⅰ Pale green	859	523	1511
⊥ Green	861	3363	1602
Fawn*	942	738	2013
■ Black	403	310	Black

Backstitching

White*, fawn*, blue metallic* and pale blue metallic* are used for backstitching only. The eye highlight is in white and the eye outline and mouth are in black; fawn is used for sand; the underside of the fish is back-stitched in brownish orange; the upper water is pale blue metallic, and lower water is blue metallic, and green is used for the waterweed stems.

———— Underside of fish, eye and mouth, upper water and waterweed stems

..... Lower water

‒ ‒ ‒ Sand

WILD ANIMALS

To portray animals in cross stitch, it is generally necessary to capture them on film first. The trouble with animals, however, is that they rarely remain still, and wild species can prove particularly elusive. This chapter examines how to obtain good, clear reference photographs, and suggests ways of adding touches of background detail to set the scene for an animal portrait.

· PHOTOGRAPHING WILDLIFE ·

Wildlife park or zoo

Photographs of animals play a very important part in my work. Designing wildlife embroideries from sketches and drawings found in books is a very good way to start, and indeed it is the only way of 'capturing' some creatures in cross stitch, but designing from your own photographs will give you a very special sense of achievement.

The best place to begin is probably at a zoo or a wildlife park, where the animals are contained, and where they are used to human contact and being photographed – indeed some appear to enjoy having their photographs taken. Wire netting and bars are a problem in some zoos, but remember that a reference picture for a cross stitch design need not be a prize-winning photograph. Bars, branches and bits of other animals can all be taken out when you come to the drawing stage of your design.

When taking photographs of animals, follow the guidelines given below.

- Try to get as close to the animal as possible.
- Keep the camera steady and focus it as accurately as you can.
- Always get the animal's eyes sharp – clear, expressive eyes make a successful picture.
- Choose a bright day for taking your photographs – good light brings out all the colours in an animal's coat.
- When you go out photographing for your design work, go alone, or with some other like-minded person. There is nothing worse than being hurried along by a group of people who just want to take a quick look at the animals and move on.

Whatever animal you want to photograph, you will need patience and perseverance, especially if you have your heart set on a particular species. No amount of expensive camera equipment will replace the need for these two qualities. In a zoo or wildlife park there are always some animals awake and alert, and it is best to concentrate on these first. When I visited a wildlife park in Scotland, I remember spending hours waiting for the badgers to wake up. Being nocturnal, they were very sleepy, but they emerged from their sett just before the park was due to close. I managed to find a chink in the netting which surrounded their enclosure, and through this I was able to point the camera lens – the resulting photographs were the basis of the badger design on pages 84–5.

Photographing wildlife in your garden

If you want to photograph wild animals in your own garden, the key is patience. Animals tend

to come to places where they can find food, so feed them regularly. Grey squirrels are no problem, because they will become so tame that they will take food from your hand, as many do from visitors in public parks and gardens.

We feed the foxes that visit our garden every night on scraps. They enjoy fruity treats, such as tarts and jam sandwiches, as well as savoury snacks, and if we are really short of food for them, they will always appreciate an egg. It is a delight to see a fox carry an egg in his mouth without breaking it.

Hedgehogs like dog meat and meaty bones to gnaw. They love bread and milk, but it is not good for them, and should be offered only very sparingly, if at all.

Woodmice love finely grated cheese and little bits of fruit cut into tiny pieces.

It is best to set up your wildlife feeding station close to a window from which you can watch the comings and goings. Daylight photography is no more difficult than in a wildlife park, but many wild animals are nocturnal. They quickly get used to the click and the flash of a camera, however, and will carry on eating without turning a hair. You can also work from a hide in the garden, but I prefer a bit of comfort! Enjoy your photography.

Useful tips
- Place the food in the same place every night so the animals get used to coming to a particular spot.
- If you have an outside light, leave it on, so your wild visitors get used to it. They also quickly adapt to security lights. Light enables you to see the animal clearly, and to focus the camera sharply.
- Make sure that the food is placed sufficiently close to the window for you to take good close-ups.

- Always wear dark clothing, and work from a darkened room – this way, you can see the animal, but unless you make quick movements, it cannot see you.
- Before your garden visitors arrive, measure the distance from the feeding spot to the window against which your camera will be used. Adjust your focus, speed setting for flash and aperture, in readiness for the arrival of your subjects. Always have a small flashlight handy in case you need to alter your settings in the course of the evening.
- Some people prefer to use a tripod, but you may find that this hampers movement and flexibility.
- It is essential that you photograph through only one pane of glass, so double glazing should be pulled back. The camera lens should be flush against the window – otherwise you will get reflections.

· BADGER ·

1 To see a badger in the wild must be a wonderful experience, but I have only been able to observe them in captivity. The badger that appears in this design was based on one I encountered in a Scottish wildlife park. I took a number of photographs, in one of which he was drinking from a shallow pool. Since badgers are generally nocturnal, this gave me the idea of creating a night-time scene, with the badger, the silhouette of a bare tree, and moonlight shining on a pool of water. Here was a scene that cried out to be interpreted with metallic threads.

2 The design space available was worked out in exactly the same way as for the Cat portrait (see page 70).

3 As this design was embroidered on a 22-count Aida, one strand of cotton was used throughout, except where metallic threads were introduced – the blending filaments are so fine that they do not make the stitches bulky, even on a fine fabric such as this. I used the fluorescent glow-in-the-dark metallic thread for the moon, and combined the same thread with one strand of blue for the ripples in the pool – and yes, the moon in the embroidery does shine in a darkened room, and the ripples have a subdued sparkle.

4 The completed design was mounted in the card in the same way as the Cat (see page 70).

MOONLIGHT ▶	KREINIK	ANCHOR	DMC	MADEIRA
▪ White		1	Blanc	White
─ Cream (fluorescent)	052F			
⅄ Pink		868	758	0403
Ripple blue*	⎰052F	121	793	0906
(one strand of each	⎱			
I Yellowish grey		900	3024	1901
⚏ Light grey		399	318	1802
T Grey		233	414	1801
✚ Dark grey		401	413	1713
■ Black		403	310	Black

Backstitching
Backstitch the eye outline in white, the head outline and claws in black; the tail outline in light grey; the skyline, cloud edge, shore of lake, cloud around the moon and ground shading in grey, and backstitch the ripples with one thread of blue, used for backstitching only, combined with one thread of fluorescent cream.*

...... Ripples
_____ All other backstitching

· WOODMOUSE ·

The background in the photograph was drab, so in my design I drew the woodmouse on a red fly agaric toadstool, and introduced berries, a leaf and some grass.

1 The inspiration for this design came as I was sitting looking out of the dining-room window late one night. I often sit here in the dark, with only the patio light on, because all sorts of creatures pass by. Foxes come every night; hedgehogs snuffle through in the summer, and a tawny owl sometimes sits on the clothes post. On this particular night I saw something that looked like a brown leaf, caught by the breeze, and it was only when the movement stopped that I realized it was a woodmouse. Using grated cheese to tempt her, I managed to take a photograph, with the aid of the flash and my telephoto lens.

2 The design space available was worked out in exactly the same way as for the Cat portrait (see page 70).

3 The woodmouse design was embroidered with two strands of thread. For the top of the toadstool, blending filaments were substituted for one of the cotton threads when stitching the red cap and white spots, making the toadstool cap sparkle as it might on a moonlit night. I also used blending filaments to give a frosty sparkle to the berries and leaf.

4 The completed design was mounted in the card in the same way as the Cat (see page 70).

WOODMOUSE ▶		KREINIK	ANCHOR	DMC	MADEIRA
▬	White		1	Blanc	White
▪	Fluorescent white	⎰052F			
	(one strand of each)	⎱	1	Blanc	White
人	Dusky pink		893	224	0813
✔	Deep pink		10	351	0214
⊔	Very deep pink		11	350	0213
✚	Toadstool red	⎰003			
	(one strand of each)	⎱	46	666	0210
⏚	Berry red	⎰003HL			
	(one strand of each)	⎱	46	666	0210
✖	Yellow		298	972	0107
⊦	Orange		316	970	0204

⬕	Sparkly mid-green	⎰008			
	(one strand of each)	⎱	216	320	1311
⊐	Dark green		246	319	1313
▮	Golden brown	⎰215C			
	(one strand of each)	⎱	365	435	2010
❖	Pale grey		398	415	1803
T	Mid-grey		233	414	1801
◢	Dark grey		401	413	1713
■	Black		403	310	Black

Backstitching
Outline the mouse's eye in black; backstitch the feet, ears, nose and whiskers in dark grey, and the berries and leaf stalks in golden brown, and highlight the mouse's eye in white.

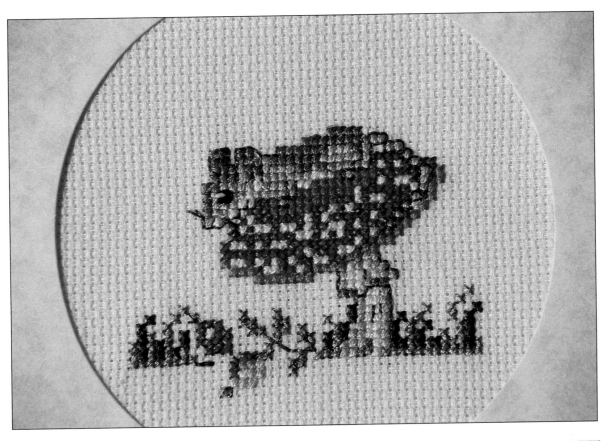

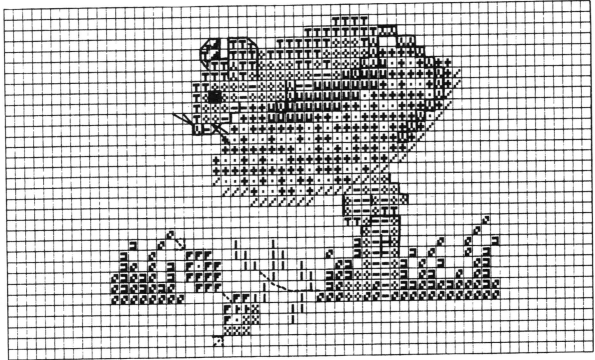

· HEDGEHOG ·

> **· YOU WILL NEED ·**
> 17cm × 5cm (6¾in × 2in) of 14-count
> cream Aida fabric • 17cm × 5cm
> (6¾in × 2in) of iron-on interfacing •
> Stranded embroidery cottons in the
> colours listed in the panel •
> Card/bookmark measuring 18cm × 5cm
> (7in × 2in), with an aperture measuring
> 13.5cm × 3cm (5¼in × 1¼in), for
> suppliers see page 128

The hedgehog design that resulted is a very simple repeat pattern – three identical animals following one another across the card. Clearly you could make further repeats to adapt the design for use as an edging pattern along one side of a place setting, along a table runner, or around the bottom of a skirt. Equally, single motifs could be embroidered on small objects such as egg cosies and key fob inserts.

2 The design space was worked out in exactly the same way as for the Cat portrait earlier (see page 70).

3 The hedgehogs were embroidered with three strands of cotton in the needle. The face of the hedgehog, with his little grey snout and bright eyes, presents no problem to the designer, but the spines are more difficult. Each one seems to be composed of three colours – creamy brown, almost black and white – and this gives the

1 Hedgehogs often run across our patio at night, but occasionally one appears in the daytime. This young one loved the worms and slugs we found for him, and I couldn't resist photographing him next to our hedgehog money box.

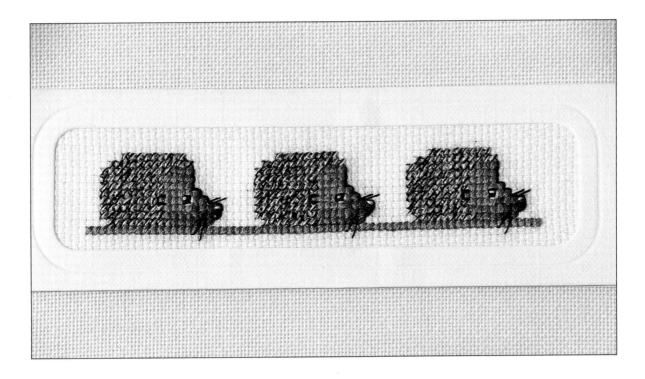

spiny coat an overall grizzled look. When the three main colours were stitched separately, the hedgehog began to look like a chequered board, so to overcome this I embroidered the spines with a combination of one strand each of white, black and light brown in the needle.

4 The completed design was mounted in the card in the same way as the Cat (see page 70).

TRIPLETS ▼	ANCHOR	DMC	MADEIRA
White	1	Blanc	White
Green	267	470	1502
Light brown	378	841	1911
Brown	379	840	1912
Dark grey	401	413	1713
Black	403	310	Black
Mixture – white, black and light brown			

Backstitching
The eye outline and highlight are backstitched in white, and the head, ears and whiskers are outlined in black.

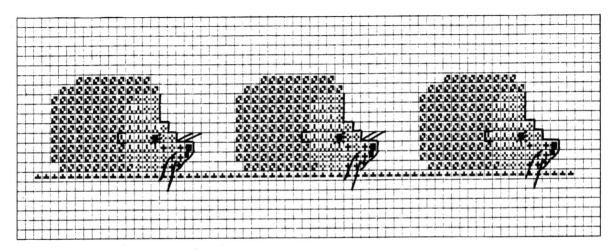

· GREY SQUIRREL ·

1 The squirrel that appears in the photograph used for this design is called Nibbles. His mother was killed by a car and Nibbles was found clinging to her, still alive, but very tiny and helpless. We adopted this orphan and he became very tame. I have lots of photographs of him but chose this particular one because it featured colourful hawthorn berries, which added a welcome splash of colour to the finished design.

2 The design space available was worked out in exactly the same way as for the Cat portrait (see page 70).

3 The embroidery was stitched with two strands of cotton in the needle, except for the berries, where a metallic blending filament was substituted for one of the cotton threads. This gave a shine to the red hawthorn berries, and two white stitches on each supplied the highlights.

4 The completed design was mounted in the card in the same way as the Cat (see page 70).

NIBBLES ▶	KREINIK	ANCHOR	DMC	MADEIRA
• White		1	Blanc	White
⅄ Pink		893	224	0813
♻ Shiny red	{003			
(one strand of each)	{	13	349	0212
I Light green		265	3348	1409
+ Green		817	3346	1407
Y Pale golden brown		362	437	2012
⊦ Golden brown		365	435	2010
⊢ Pale brown		832	612	2108
T Brown		898	611	2107
– Silver grey		397	762	1804
❖ Pale grey		399	318	1802
✕ Mid-grey		233	414	1801
⊔ Dark grey		401	413	1713
■ Black		403	310	Black

Backstitching
The eye is highlighted with one strand of white and outlined with two strands; backstitch the nose, face, whiskers, chest, feet and ears in dark grey, and the leaf and berry stalks in brown.

BIRDS AND BUTTERFLIES

Birds and butterflies make colourful and attractive subjects for cross stitch designs, but they are not the easiest creatures to photograph. Small birds are timid, secretive and usually very active, while butterflies always seem to close up their wings just as you snap your photograph. In this section, we explore ways of putting together small composite studies using a variety of sources. The resulting designs have all been embroidered on items with a teatime theme, but they could easily be adapted to other household items.

· PREPARING COMPOSITE STUDIES ·

Small birds are difficult to photograph, even in a garden, so for my bird designs I rely largely upon reference books. The best ones to use are those with good clear photographs of birds, or ones with drawings of birds in natural positions.

Having decided on the species of bird I want to feature in my design, I collect together as many pictures as I can of the bird in question, and read and make notes on its habits, food and environment. This means that I can not only draw a bird that, hopefully, can be identified, but also feature it in an appropriate setting.

When I was deciding which birds to choose for a set of table napkins, I looked for those that would form a pleasing group. I opted for the tit family because they are familiar and very popular little birds. They vary in colour and appearance, but they are all small acrobatic birds that can be depicted in a variety of positions. The individual species occupy a

black cap and breast stripe
green back
bluish wings
white bar
pussy willow
yellow breast

GREAT TIT *Parus major*

range of habitats, and this gave me the opportunity to draw each bird with a different twig or branch characteristic of its environment. In the case of the four types of tit which frequent my own garden, I chose the shrubs and trees in which I am accustomed to seeing them perch and feed. For the crested tit, I gathered a twig of pine from the park, and for the willow tit, I found a frond of willow with yellow-brown catkins.

Thus my bird designs are based on composite drawings researched from a variety of books on birds and plants, as well as from some live plant specimens. The six species featured on the set are listed below.

Blue tit · This is probably the most familiar and best-loved member of the tit family. Though it is a woodland bird, most of us encounter the blue tit in our gardens, where it visits bird tables and feeds from hanging peanut dispensers. I drew my blue tit on a twig of common hazel, because I often see these little birds hanging precariously from twigs of hazel, projecting from the hedge around our local park. To my mind, the little red

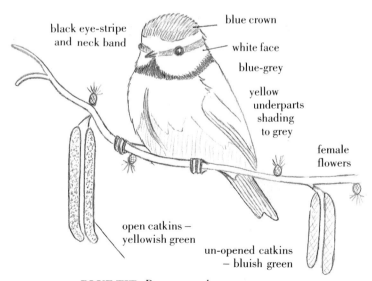

black eye-stripe and neck band
blue crown
white face
blue-grey
yellow underparts shading to grey
female flowers
open catkins – yellowish green
un-opened catkins – bluish green

BLUE TIT *Parus caeruleus*

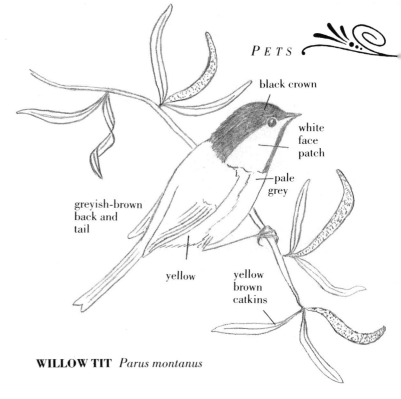

female flowers added just the touch of brightness needed to complete the design.

Great tit The largest species in the tit family, this handsome bird is found in woodlands, agricultural areas, and in urban gardens. It feeds on a variety of foods, ranging from spring buds, fruits, seeds and berries to weavils, spiders and insects. I chose to draw my great tit on a twig of pussy willow, just as we see him every spring in our front garden.

Coal tit The smallest of the British tits, this is only half the weight of a great tit. These little birds like all sorts of woodlands as well as orchards and gardens. They eat beetles, flies, moths, insects, spiders and various seeds. They also feed from garden bird tables. The relatively long slender beak is ideal for winkling out insects from the spring blossoms, and we frequently see them in our cherry tree in the spring.

Willow tit The willow tit likes damp woodlands of willow, birch and alder trees. It hunts for insects, insect eggs and larvae in the lower branches of trees and shrubs. I drew my

WILLOW TIT *Parus montanus*

bird on a flimsy willow branch, with some yellow brown catkins among the slender leaves.

Long-tailed tit This bird is easily identified by its black, white and pink plumage, and its long tail. It lives mainly on the edge of wooded areas, and in woodland clearings. We occasionally see long-tailed tits in our garden, hopping from twig to twig in the species rose bed, searching for insects and spiders.

COAL TIT *Parus ater*

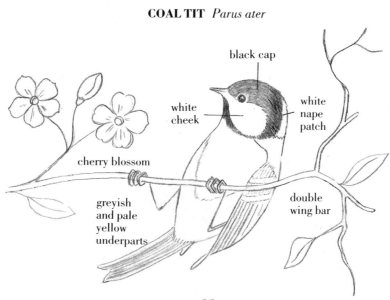

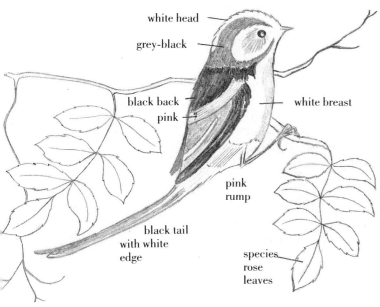

white head
grey-black
black back
pink
white breast
pink rump
black tail with white edge
species rose leaves

LONG-TAILED TIT *Aegithalos caudatus*

Crested tit These are present through much of Europe, but are found only in a relatively small area of Britain, in the pine forests of the Scottish Highlands around the Spey valley. They feed among the pine foliage, and on the trunks of trees as well as on the ground. Their fine beaks are well adapted to extracting insects from clusters of pine needles and the seeds from pine cones.

Back Stitch

Simple back stitch is widely used by cross stitchers to outline motifs, and to make them stand out boldly. It is often worked in black, which is too stark for my taste. I do use back stitch, however, to add fine detail, to highlight, or to emphasize part of a line which would otherwise be lost against the background.

In all the designs in this book there is some backstitching, but I always try to keep it to a minimum. In my series of bird designs, I use back stitch frequently, but not extensively.

Eyes Small birds' eyes are always bright, but otherwise inconspicuous, perhaps a ploy to safeguard them against injury by predators. Four out of the six tits chosen for these designs have their eyes on the margin between black and white face feathers, which means that if the eyes are going to be seen on an embroidery they have to be outlined, either partially or wholly, in a colour which will make them more prominent. For these birds, I used white, as it formed a natural continuation of the white cheek feathers. Sometimes white looks a little glaring, however, and against brown feathers, you may prefer ecru or cream. For certain birds, yellow or orange is appropriate.

Wherever possible, I like to use an eye

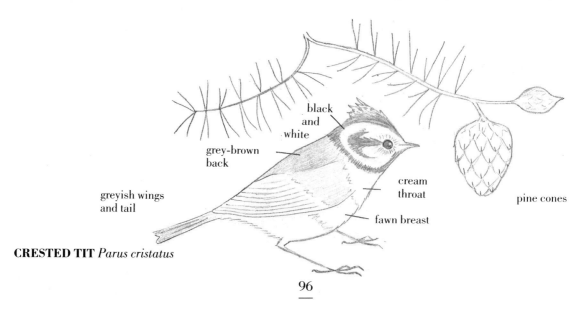

black and white
grey-brown back
greyish wings and tail
cream throat
fawn breast
pine cones

CRESTED TIT *Parus cristatus*

highlight in white or ecru – just a tiny backstitch on the eye itself. It is amazing how this brings a bird or any creature to life.

Legs All small birds have very fragile legs and claws. It would be impossible to work these in cross stitch – unless you were working on a very large scale. The important thing here is to get the position and angle of the legs correct, and the tiny claws in as lifelike a position as possible. I never try to do this from memory, but refer to the birds hopping about in the garden – the legs are always set further back on the body than I imagine. Most small garden birds have three forward-facing toes and a hind claw for perching – except for woodpeckers, which have two toes facing forward and two behind. If you want your design to be authentic, it is important to get such details correct.

Other parts of the bird Backstitching is also useful for making clear a particular line which would otherwise be very pale. Sometimes it is appropriate to use black; for example, to show the dark shadow under the wing of the crested tit. Often, however, a paler colour will show the limits of a white or pale grey area more effectively. For example, black would have been rather heavy as an outline for the nape of the coal tit's neck, or the long-tailed tit's throat, and so I opted for grey.

Details of flowers and plants Backstitching is ideal for adding the final detailed touches to flowers and plants – for example, the little red flowers on the hazel twigs, the calyx of each pussy willow floret, the centres of small flowers, or simply the stalks and veins of leaves, or the needles of a pine twig.

My advice, therefore, is to use back stitch with discrimination, and make every stitch serve a real purpose in the promotion of the design.

· BIRD NAPKINS ·

• YOU WILL NEED •
For each table napkin, measuring 40.5cm (16in) square, including a 12mm (½in) fringe all around:

Either a ready-prepared napkin (for suppliers, see page 128) or a 45cm (18in) square of 28-count cream evenweave fabric • Stranded embroidery cottons, as listed with the individual designs

Making the napkins
Measure in from the corner and place the centre of the design at the same spacing for each napkin, remembering to allow for trimming and fringing if you are making your own.

For all cross stitch, use three strands of thread and work over two fabric threads; use two strands of thread for backstitching.

If you are making your own napkins, trim each one to measure 40.5cm (16in) square. Either stitch by machine or hemstitch by hand all around, 12mm (½in) in from the edges, and then remove threads to complete the fringe.

BLUE TIT ▼		ANCHOR	DMC	MADEIRA
▪	White	1	Blanc	White
	Red*	335	606	0209
I	Light yellow	293	727	0110
Y	Yellow	289	307	0104
❖	Blue	131	798	0911
✎	Light grey blue	921	931	1711
✚	Grey blue	922	930	1712
⅄	Pale green	266	471	1501
⊥	Blue green	216	320	1311

		ANCHOR	DMC	MADEIRA
T	Grey green	859	522	1512
✖	Brown	898	611	2107
⊥	Pale grey	398	415	1803
☙	Dark grey	401	413	1713
U	Black	403	310	Black

Backstitching
Backstitch the eyes and beak in white; the legs and claws in black; the stems of the short catkins in blue green and those of the longer catkins in pale green, and the hazel flowers in red (used for backstitching only).*

GREAT TIT ▼	ANCHOR	DMC	MADEIRA
· White	1	Blanc	White
⅄ Pale yellow	293	727	0110
— Lemon	288	445	0103
♣ Grey blue	850	926	1707
✚ Dark grey blue	851	924	1706
▱ Greyish green	859	522	1512
T Ginger brown	371	433	2008

✕ Brown	889	610	2105
I Pale grey	397	762	1804
⊥ Grey	233	414	1801
■ Black	403	310	Black

Backstitching

Backstitch the eye and highlight in white; the legs, claws, and base of the willow calyx in black, and the twiglets bearing the pussy willow florets in brown.

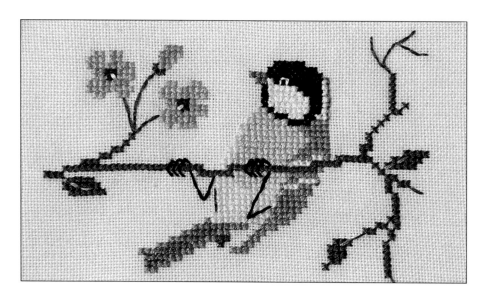

COAL TIT ▼	ANCHOR	DMC	MADEIRA
▪ White	1	Blanc	White
⊱ Pale pink	50	605	0613
┥ Pink	75	604	0614
ᴜ Maroon	70	3685	0602
— Lemon	288	445	0103
⅄ Yellow	293	727	0110
❖ Grey blue	850	926	1707
✛ Dark blue	851	924	1706
ᴚ Greyish green	859	522	1512
T Dark green	862	520	1514

	ANCHOR	DMC	MADEIRA
✖ Brown	889	610	2105
I Pale grey	397	762	1804
⊥ Mid-grey	233	414	1801
⊐ Dark grey	400	317	1714
■ Black	403	310	Black

Backstitching

Backstitch the eye and the flower centres in white; the legs and claws in black; the back of the bird's head in mid-grey; and leaf veins in greyish green; the blossom stalks and twigs in brown; the lower body in dark blue, and the back of the wing in grey blue.

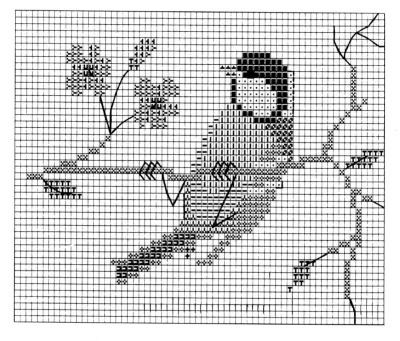

WILLOW TIT ▼	ANCHOR	DMC	MADEIRA
▪ White	1	Blanc	White
❖ Yellow	891	676	2208
➕ Greenish yellow	280	733	1611
Lemon	293	727	0110
(use one strand of greenish yellow and two strands of lemon)			
◪ Yellowish green	266	471	1501
⬚ Yellowish brown	898	370	2112

I Light fawn	392	642	1906
T Fawn	903	640	1905
✖ Brown	898	611	2107
— Light grey	397	762	1804
⊥ Grey	233	414	1801
■ Black	403	310	Black

Backstitching

Backstitch the top of the eyes and the highlight in white, and the legs and claws in black.

LONG-TAILED TIT ▼	ANCHOR	DMC	MADEIRA
• White	1	Blanc	White
⅄ Pale dusky pink	933	543	1909
♣ Dusky pink	893	224	0813
Pale green*	265	3348	1409
+ Green	817	3346	1407
⊔ Brown	889	610	2105
− Pale grey	398	415	1803
⅄ Dark grey	401	413	1713
■ Black	403	310	Black

Backstitching
*Backstitch the eye highlight in white; the legs, claws and throat
in dark grey; the twigs in brown, and the leaf stalks and veins in
pale green* (used only for backstitching).*

CRESTED TIT ▼	ANCHOR	DMC	MADEIRA
• White	1	Blanc	White
— Cream	387	712	2101
Dark green*	862	520	1514
⊣ Fawn	372	422	2102
⅄ Greyish fawn	956	613	2109
♣ Pale greyish brown	392	642	1906
♣ Greyish brown	903	640	1905
✚ Ginger brown	944	869	2105
T Brown	889	610	2105

⊔ Dark brown	905	3031	2003
I Pale grey	397	762	1804
◆ Greenish grey	8581	646	1812
✖ Dark greenish grey	905	645	1811
■ Black	403	310	Black

Backstitching

Backstitch the eye highlight in white; the wings, legs and claws in black, and the pine needles in dark green* (used for backstitching only).

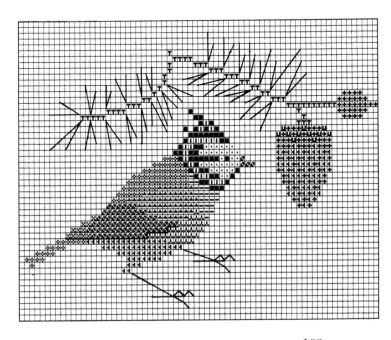

· KINGFISHER CLOCK ·

· YOU WILL NEED ·

For the clock, measuring 165cm × 12.5cm (6½in × 5in):

21.5cm × 18cm (8½in × 7in) of 18-count cream Aida fabric • 21.5cm × 18cm (8½in × 7in) iron-on interfacing • Stranded embroidery cottons and Hi-lustre metallics, in the colours listed in the panel • Perspex cathedral clock, see page 128 for suppliers

This design was developed from a photograph in the usual way, the main task being to choose threads that would convey the brilliant colours of the live bird. Hi-lustre metallics, blended with ordinary stranded cotton (one thread of each) seemed to me particularly appropriate for parts of the bird, the dragonfly and the fish. If, however, you prefer to work the design in stranded cotton only, simply use two threads of this in the needle throughout.

I could not find the exact shade of deep blue required for the nape of the kingfisher's neck, so I combined one strand each of two different blues. For the kingfisher's back and wing edges, I used a strand of green and one of blue to produce the dark greeny-blue colour I wanted.

Backstitch is used to create the ripples and water droplets on the river, and for other fine details. I also decided to backstitch the dragonfly's wings, which are almost transparent; cross stitch would have looked too heavy.

Assembling the clock

The line around the chart indicates the clock edge, but it is only approximate, and the final adjustment is critical. Do not attempt to cut your material to size until the finished embroidery has been backed with interfacing.

Slide the finished design down between the two plates of perspex for a trial run. Measure carefully how much you need to cut off the bottom to bring your spindle hole down to match that in the perspex. Once you have got this right, trim the embroidery to fit the shape of the clock exactly. Using a sharp craft knife, cut out the hole for the clock spindle, then follow the maker's instructions for assembly.

KINGFISHER ▶		KREINIK (HL)	ANCHOR	DMC	MADEIRA
·	White		1	Blanc	White
◩	Dark orange		326	720	0309
↗	Kingfisher blue		168	597	1110
⊥	Blue metallic	014HL			
	(one strand of each)		168	597	1110
✚	Deep blue		132	797	0912
	(one strand of each)		168	597	1110
✖	Dark blue	051HL			
	(one strand of each)		132	797	0912
⊔	Dark greeny blue		132	797	0912
	(one strand of each)		189	991	1204
◄	Pale green		266	471	1501
✧	Mid-green		267	469	1503
⊓	Dark green		246	319	1313
⌐	Light grey green		859	3053	1510
⊥	Dark grey green		846	3051	1508
I	Creamy fawn		942	738	2013
⋏	Fawn		832	612	2108
Y	Light tan		363	402	2307
⊢	Light orange brown		307	977	2301
T	Orange brown		308	976	2302
F	Dark orange brown		324	922	0310
↵	Mid-brown		889	610	2105
⊏	Dark brown		382	3021	1904
−	Pale grey		398	415	1803
↘	Dark grey		401	413	1713
⊣	Dark grey metallic	011HL			
	(one strand of each)		401	413	1713
■	Black		403	310	Black

Backstitching
Use white for the bird and fish eye highlights and the outline of the bird's eye; dark grey for outline of the bird's face; mid-green for the leaf; kingfisher blue for the ripples and water droplets; mid-brown for branch, and dark grey metallic for the dragonfly wings.

Note The line shown here indicating the clock edge is only approximate, as the final adjustment is very critical. *Do not cut your material* until you have actually slipped it into the mount, and lined up the spindle hole with the marker on your material.

DESIGNING YOUR OWN CATHEDRAL
· CLOCK ·

The perspex clock has been made to suit any cross stitch design worked on Aida or linen, so you can use a ready-made design, or create your own. If your fabric has a stitch count other than either the 18-count shown here, or 14-count (where the chart is provided with the clock), you will need to re-calculate the position of the hour marks, or numerals on the face.

· YOU WILL NEED ·
A large sheet of graph paper • A ruler •
A protractor • Sharp pencil and eraser

---

1 Establish the count of the material you intend to use, and work out the number of squares/stitches at your disposal, horizontally and vertically. Measure the width of the shaped off-cuts from the top left and right of the clock, and draw these in as carefully as possible.

2 Calculate, as accurately as possible, the location of the centre of the spindle aperture and mark it clearly on your graph paper.

3 Using a protractor, position it on the centre of the spindle hole, and accurately mark off points at 30 degree intervals. Make sure that one of these points is directly above the spindle (12 o'clock), one is directly below the spindle (6 o'clock) and that the 9 o'clock point and the 3 o'clock point form a straight line with the centre of the spindle hole, parallel to the bottom edge of the clock.

4 From the centre of the spindle hole, draw in the twelve radiating lines up to the edge of the pattern. Your numerals or hour spots must be placed accurately on these lines, otherwise the hand will not point precisely to the hours.

5 It is more pleasing to the eye if the hour spots form a symmetrical pattern, but they need not be equidistant from the spindle hole. You may prefer to place them around the edge of the clock to allow maximum space for your design.

6 If you are going to use Roman numerals, remember that 4 o'clock is shown as IIII on all clock faces with Roman numerals, rather than IV, which for any timepiece is considered incorrect.

7 Create your design to fit into the remaining space.

8 Fit your embroidery into the clock face, following the maker's instructions.

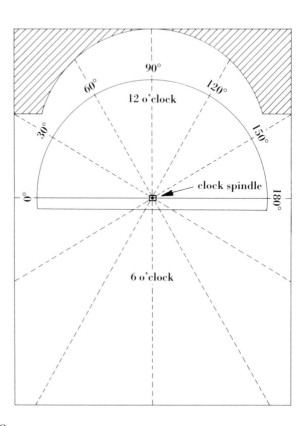

· BUTTERFLY POT COVERS ·

• YOU WILL NEED •

For each cover, measuring 16.5cm
(6½in) in diameter, including the
lace edging:

18cm (7in) square of 18-count cream
Aida fabric • Stranded cottons, as listed
in the appropriate panel • 70cm (¾yd)
of lace, 12mm (½in) wide, for trimming •
1m (1yd) of narrow ribbon in a colour of
your choice • Jar with a top 6.25cm
(2½in) in diameter

I chose the Comma butterfly and the Painted Lady butterfly as the subjects for my teatime jam pot covers, because both species are attracted by fruit. These embroideries were designed in spring, so in the absence of live specimens the raspberries and strawberries had to be adapted from pictures on the fruit pages of my gardening magazines.

The comma occurs throughout Europe, and across to China and Japan. This butterfly, with its irregular outline and leaflike underside, is able to merge into the vegetation when it closes its wings, but when it opens them in bright sunshine it is a lovely sight. Commas are active in our garden from the first warm days of spring to the last balmy days of autumn whenever the sun shines. They are attracted especially to the ripe plums, raspberries and apples in our fruit garden.

The painted lady is distributed world-wide – with the exception of South America – but we never see it in our garden! It is a fast-flying, migrant species, which cannot survive northern winters. In spring it moves north from its winter grounds in Africa, southern Europe, and the southern United States. For my initial drawings and the choice of colours for this design, I have had to rely on reference books.

Making the covers
Both covers are made in the same way. Complete the embroidery, using two threads of stranded cotton. Take a pair of compasses and place the point in the exact centre of the design. Mark out a circle with a radius of 7cm (2¾in). If you have no compasses, you can use a suitable plate, but it is difficult to centre the design with this method.

Carefully cut out your circle of material and overlock the edges with machine stitching. Join the short edges of the lace together with a tiny french seam and hand-stitch the lace around the edge, frilling it slightly.

Fill your jar with jam and place the cover over the top. Secure with the ribbon, make a neat bow to give an attractive finish.

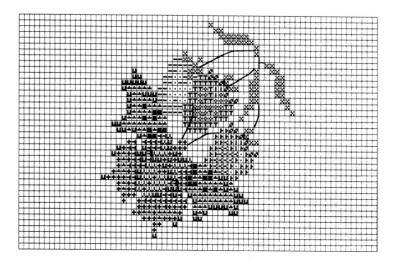

COMMA ▲	ANCHOR	DMC	MADEIRA
◄ Pink	9	760	0405
⊢ Peach	10	352	0303
▪ Light yellow	886	677	2207
⊥ Light orange	307	977	2301
❖ Purplish red	42	3350	0603
T Dull Maroon	896	315	0810
⅄ Light brown	901	680	2212
⊣ Yellow brown	308	782	2212
✦ Brown	944	869	2105
Ц Dark brown	905	3031	2003
■ Very dark brown	382	3371	2004
I Pale green	264	472	1414
– Light green	887	372	2110
◧ Mid-green	266	471	1501
✕ Dark green	267	469	1503

Backstitching

Backstitch the stalks in dark green; the right fruit highlights in pink, and the antennae and wings in a very dark brown.

PAINTED LADY ▼	ANCHOR	DMC	MADEIRA
▪ White	1	Blanc	White
⊢ Peach	10	352	0303
❖ Red	46	349	0212
T Dark red	13	347	0407
⊥ Light orange	307	977	2301
◧ Dull orange	308	976	2302
⅄ Light brown	901	680	2212
✦ Brown	944	869	2105
Ц Dark brown	905	3031	2003
I Pale green	264	472	1414
✕ Dark green	267	469	1503
■ Black	403	310	Black

Backstitching

Backstitch the antennae in black and the fruit stalks in dark green.

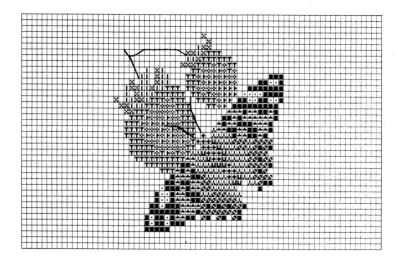

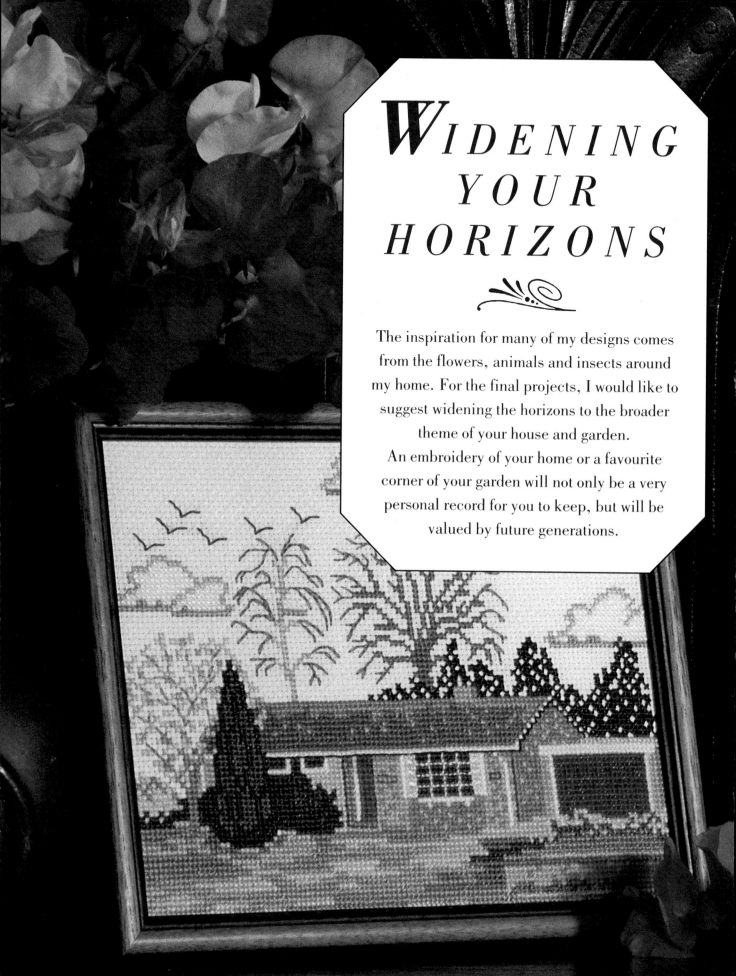

WIDENING YOUR HORIZONS

The inspiration for many of my designs comes from the flowers, animals and insects around my home. For the final projects, I would like to suggest widening the horizons to the broader theme of your house and garden.

An embroidery of your home or a favourite corner of your garden will not only be a very personal record for you to keep, but will be valued by future generations.

· AN EMBROIDERY OF YOUR HOME ·

· Y O U   W I L L   N E E D ·
*To make a cross stitch of your
own home:*

A good photograph • Clear acetate film •
Black fibre-tip pen for drawing on
acetate • Masking tape • Other design
equipment as listed on page 121

*For the embroidery featured here,
finished size 22cm × 15cm
(8½in × 5¾in) excluding the frame:*

32cm × 25cm (14½in × 10in) of 14-
count pale blue Aida fabric • Stranded
embroidery cottons, as listed in the
panel on page 121 • Frame of
your choice

The photograph

You do not have to own an expensive camera to
take a good clear photograph of your home.
Unlike so many of the subjects I have chosen for
this book, a house is a relatively permanent
structure and you can choose your day, and
the season of the year – whenever your home
looks at its best. I chose a fine spring day when
the daffodils, the forsythia and the pink blossom
of the ornamental prunus lent a touch of fresh
colour to the picture. You may prefer summer,
when your garden is ablaze with colourful
blooms, or autumn with its russet, brown and
golden tints. Even a winter shot, taken when
your home is blanketed with snow, can look
attractive. If you have the time, it is a good idea
to make four small studies, one for each season
of the year, and frame them as a large picture
or sampler.

The angle

When you have chosen the day for your
photograph, give some thought to the angle of
your picture. A shot taken straight from the front
may be the easiest one from which to do your
drawing, and subsequently your embroidery,
but it may not be the most pleasing angle.

Spend some time looking at your subject
through the camera lens until you are sure that
you have located the best viewpoint. You may
have to compose your photograph in such a way
that large shrubs and trees frame, or stand to
the side of, your picture. On the other hand,
lamp posts and telephone wires may look
unsightly on a photograph, but remember that
these can be left out of your drawing and the
final embroidery.

Depth

It is desirable to have some foreground interest
in your picture in order to give depth to your
work. This could be provided by a wall, a
shrub, or a few flowers, and if nothing
immediately presents itself to you, you can
always cheat a little when you make a drawing
of the photograph, emphasizing one of the
foreground features to make it more prominent.

The size of your photograph

I designed the embroidery of my bungalow from
a standard 15cm × 10cm (6in × 4in) colour
print. You may choose to go to the expense of
enlarging your photograph. Assuming that the
enlargement is now the size that you want your
embroidery to be, this will reduce the amount of
drawing you will need to do during the design
stage, but it is a much more costly option.

Making a design

1 Once you have obtained a good photograph,
the next stage is to convert this into a design.

Either draw a grid onto an acetate sheet (top right), using a black, permanent ink, overhead-projector pen. (You can use a non-permanent pen, in which case you will be able to re-use your acetate, but the lines will tend to smudge.) Place the grid over the photograph, and enlarge directly onto the drawing paper (right); *or* trace the main lines from the photograph on to the acetate sheet, place the grid on top, and then enlarge onto the drawing paper (bottom left).

Right The enlarged drawing is now ready to be transferred to graph tracing paper.

Place your photograph on a drawing board or similar flat surface, and secure a piece of clear acetate film over it, using masking tape. Using a black fibre-tip pen of the type intended for use with an overhead projector, and available from good stationers, trace the main outlines of the house, lawns and paths, and shrubs and trees.

2 If you have enlarged your photograph to the correct size for the finished embroidery, you will be able to omit the scaling-up stage described next. My own photograph was too small and I wanted to enlarge it to twice its size, so I next drew a line around the outer edge and then divided the area up with a grid of 12 squares across by eight down.

On a sheet of drawing paper, I drew another 12 × 8 square grid, with squares twice the size (2.5cm/1in, instead of 12mm/½in). The main lines of the design were then transferred, square by square, from the acetate film to the larger grid. I now had a drawing twice the size of the photograph, and all the proportions were accurate.

3 Next, I placed a piece of graph tracing paper over my enlarged drawing and taped it down. I transferred the main lines to the graph tracing paper, but this time I followed the horizontal and vertical lines of the graph grid. The picture was now divided into broad areas, and I had the basis of my pattern.

4 The graph paper was then taped to a piece of plain paper so that I could see the lines clearly.

5 I now chose my skeins of stranded cotton. For some sections – for example, the walls of the bungalow – I chose two or more colours, because within the broad area more detail was to be added as I stitched.

6 I chose a very pale 14-count Aida for my picture. This colour, I felt, would suggest a blue sky background without the need for any stitching. On this count, my finished embroidery would be approximately 22cm × 15cm (8½in × 5¾in).

7 Each area was stitched separately, with careful reference to the photograph. It was necessary to simplify some features to make the design workable. Not every brick, for example,

could be shown, but a suggestion of bricks could be made by distributing a few stitches of a lighter or darker colour among those in the main shade used for the walls. The shades of shrubs and conifers had to be simplified, and the tangle of branches belonging to the larger, background trees had to be eliminated, with only the general outline of some of the more prominent trees being retained.

Some shadows, the cause of which was not included in the picture, could be eliminated. I did, however, retain the dappling effect of shadows from the oak tree on the drive. The oak tree is to the right of the drive, just out of the photograph, but if I had dispensed with the shadows it cast, the drive would have presented a broad uninterrupted grey area in the foreground, and this would not have been very attractive.

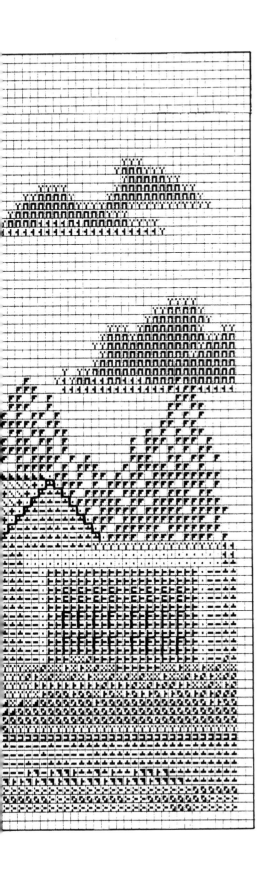

BUNGALOW ◄	ANCHOR	DMC	MADEIRA
⌐ White	1	Blanc	White
Ecru*	926	Ecru	Ecru
⅄ Cream	886	3047	2205
− Pale dusky pink	893	224	0813
⊥ Dusky pink	894	223	0812
⊰ Pink	49	3689	0607
⊤ Deep pink	66	3688	0605
⊣ Deep mauve	110	208	0804
∂ Yellow	301	744	0112
✕ Deep yellow	297	743	0113
✗ Yellowish green	268	937	1504
⊢ Blue green	878	501	1704
⌐ Dark blue green	879	500	1705
⊢ Pale green	265	3348	1409
⊾ Green	266	3347	1408
⊿ Dark green	246	3345	1406
✦ Bright green	242	989	1401
∪ Deep green	862	935	1505
∣ Pale fawn	390	3033	2001
↖ Fawn	887	372	2110
⊥ Light reddish brown	349	301	2306
⊢ Reddish brown	352	300	2304
⊣ Light brown	903	640	1905
⊣ Light grey	399	318	1802
⊐ Grey	400	317	1714
⊏ Dark grey	401	413	1713
Y Silver grey	398	415	1803
⊾ Light greenish grey	8581	647	1813
✛ Greenish grey	273	646	1812
Black*	403	310	Black

Backstitching

Backstitch the bay windows in ecru* and under the eaves in black* (both of these are used for backstitching only); the garage door, front door and porch, house number plaques, corner of the bungalow, and birds in dark grey; the twigs of large trees in light brown, and the Prunus twigs in light greenish grey.

121

· A GARDEN EMBROIDERY ·

Many people are attracted by the idea of creating a cross stitch embroidery of their own garden. A favourite part of my garden in spring is a small corner near the side gate, which is carpeted with bright yellow daffodils. I took a photograph of this area on the same day that I photographed the front of the bungalow. It was mid-afternoon, and the sun was shining into this shady corner beneath the oak tree.

———

• Y O U W I L L N E E D •
For the garden embroidery, finished size 22cm × 15cm (8½in × 5¾in), excluding the frame:

32cm × 25cm (14½in × 10in) of 16-count cream Aida fabric • Stranded cottons, as listed in the panel on page 124 • Light green fabric dye • Air brush • Frame of your choice

lovely circular opening, and we congratulated the workman on how good it looked. Arriving home later, we were horrified to find that he had carefully bricked up the aperture. We hadn't the heart to tell him that we had wanted it left as a porthole, but my design shows the opening as it was intended to be. I have omitted the garden shed, as this spoilt the view through the gate and the hole in the wall.

The daffodils closest to the wall are too small to show in any detail, but I wanted some foreground interest, so I exaggerated the difference in size between the daffodils in the foreground and those further away.

1 The garden picture was designed from a photograph in much the same way as the house picture, but I adapted the photograph in order to make the ornamental wall form a back drop to the picture. On the photograph, this wall is at a slight angle to the observer, but to make the design more straightforward, I drew it at a right angle to the observer, and also brought it further forward, which enabled me to show its structure in more detail.

When this wall was being built, we asked the bricklayer to design a porthole in it. When we went out in the early afternoon, there was a

2 This embroidery has been worked on 16-count cream Aida fabric which has been sprayed with a pale green fabric paint. Daffodils, like all yellow flowers, are very difficult to embroider effectively. On cream or pale-coloured fabrics they are lost completely unless you add extensive back stitching, and this, I feel, can destroy the delicacy of the flowers. Here, I have used one strand of a dark green thread for the backstitching.

3 Two threads of stranded cotton were used in the needle for all the cross stitching. The gate was embroidered in back stitch, since the fine wrought-ironwork would have looked much too heavy in cross stitch. The back stitch on the gate was worked with two strands of cotton, but the back stitch used for other fine details was stitched with only one strand in the needle.

Completing your house and garden pictures

The sizes of your finished pictures will depend on the sizes of your original photographs and of your drawings, as well as the count of material you choose to use for your embroideries. Whatever the sizes of your finished pictures, however, ensure that you allow an adequate margin of fabric around them. The embroideries should be carefully stretched over mounting cards and laced across the back, before they are inserted into their frames.

GARDEN ▶		ANCHOR	DMC	MADEIRA
▬	Pale pink	892	225	0814
✚	Purplish pink	896	315	0810
⅄	Light dusky pink	893	224	0813
✕	Dusky pink	894	223	0812
▐	Pale lemon	300	745	0111
⅃•	Lemon	301	744	0112
⌐	Yellow	297	743	0113
⊤	Deep yellow	303	742	0114
⊏	Blue green	878	501	1704
⊥	Green	260	3364	1603
∏	Dark green	262	3363	1602

♣	Fawn	372	422	2102
	Deep fawn*	905	3031	2003
➘	Reddish brown	341	355	0401
•	Pale grey	234	762	1804
	Grey*	400	317	1714

Backstitching
Use grey* for the ornamental blocks and path, and deep fawn* for the daffodil trumpets and lines separating the petals (both of these colours are used for backstitching only); purplish pink for the hole in the wall; reddish brown for the gate; blue green for the daffodil stalks, and dark green to outline the daffodil heads and buds.

· BASIC STITCHES ·

Cross stitch

To make a cross stitch, bring the needle up from the back of the material at the point at which you wish to begin. Carefully hold the end of the thread as you pull your needle through, and secure the loose end with your first five or six stitches. Never begin with a knot.

For a single cross stitch, as shown below, bring the needle up at 1, down at 2, up at 3 and down at 4.

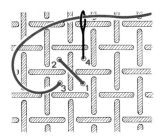

For stitching rows of cross stitch – stitch all the way across, making a row of diagonal stitches, as shown, and then work back, completing each stitch in turn.

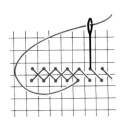
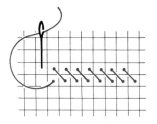

Whether you are making single cross stitches or rows of cross stitches, ensure that all stitches cross in the same direction.

Three-quarter stitch

This stitch is used to round off sharp corners and produce smooth curves. On a chart the symbol covers only half a square, and a line runs diagonally across the square to indicate which part of the square is occupied by the three-quarter stitch. One stitch is made diagonally in the same direction as this line on the chart and half a stitch is made from one of the other two corners to the centre of the square to match the half of the square that the symbol occupies. Too many three-quarter stitches make a pattern very complicated to work, and therefore they should be used with care.

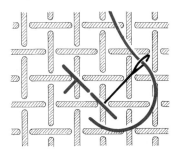

Back stitch

Back stitch is used to emphasize a particular line or to add fine detail to a design. The stitches are either worked as continuous straight lines parallel with the threads of the material, or they are worked diagonally.

To make a stitch, push the needle up through the material from the back of your work and down through the fabric one stitch length behind the first point. Pass the needle under the material, and then up one stitch length ahead of the first point.

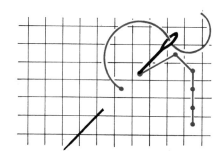

INDEX

Acorn spectacle case, 27
Aida fabrics, 40

Backstitch, 126
    flowers and plants, details
        of, 97
    motifs, outlining, 96
Badger, 84, 85
Bellpull, 52-4
Berry design, 43, 44
Birds design, 43, 44
Birds
    blue tit, 94, 98
    coal tit, 95, 100
    composite studies, 94
    crested tit, 96, 103
    eyes, 96
    great tit, 95, 99
    kingfisher clock, 106, 107
    legs, 97
    long-tailed tit, 95, 102
    napkins, 97-103
    willow tit, 95, 101
Blue tit, 94, 98
Butterfly pot covers, 111, 112

Cathedral clock, 108
Cat portrait, 70-72
Coal tit, 95, 100
Colours
    fabrics, of, 51
    interpretation of, 6
    pet designs, 68
    selecting, 30
Composite studies, 94
Crested tit, 96, 103
Cross stitch, 126
Cushion, mushroom, 29-37

Designing to scale, 41
Design, tools for, 8, 9
Dog portrait, 73-4

Evenweave fabrics, 40

Fabrics
    Aida, 40
    colours, 51
    evenweaves, 40
    silk gauze, 40
    size, calculating, 42
Firescreen, 59-65
    autumn, 64
    spring, 60
    summer, 62
    winter, 65
Flower Threads, 6, 51
Fuchsia bellpull, 52-4

Garden, embroidery of, 122-5
Garden flowers
    bellpull, 52-4
    firescreen, 59-65
    photographs, 48
    pot pourri covers, 56
    pressed specimens, 48
    records of, 48
    sketches of, 48
    watercolours, 48
Goldfish, 76, 79
Great tit, 95, 99
Grey squirrel, 90, 91

Hedgehog, 88, 89
Home, embroidery of, 116-21

Kingfisher clock, 106, 107

Leaf designs
    leafy spray, 18-20
    motif, repeating, 16
    simple, 12, 13
    theme, developing, 15, 16
Lighting, 9
Long-tailed tit, 95, 102

Materials, 9
Metallic threads, 7, 69
Mushroom studies, 28-31

Napkins, bird, 97-103
Natural objects, drawing, 24
Nut design, 24-7

Oval frame, designing for, 42

Pet designs
    cat portrait, 70-72
    colour, applying, 68
    dog portrait, 73-4
    goldfish, 76, 79
    metallic threads, using, 69
    rabbit, 76, 78
    tinted backgrounds, 68
Photographs
    flowers, 48
    wildlife, of, 82-4
Pot pourri covers, 56

Rabbit, 76, 78
Round frame, designing for, 42

Scale, designing to, 41
Silk gauze, 40
Sketches, flowers, 48
Spray, leafy, 18-20
Stitches
    backstitch, 126
    cross stitch, 126
    three-quarter stitch, 126

Tapestry needles, 7, 9
Threads, 9, 40
    blending filaments, 69
    Flower, 6, 51
    metallic, 7, 69
Three-quarter stitch, 126
Tinted backgrounds, 68

Watercolours, flowers, 48
Wild animals
    badger, 84, 85
    grey squirrel, 90, 91
    hedgehog, 88, 89
    photographing, 82-4
    woodmouse, 86, 87
Willow tit, 95, 101
Woodmouse, 86, 87

• ACKNOWLEDGEMENTS •

I should like to thank my mother, Violet Watts, who so patiently made up or assembled all the embroidered articles illustrated in this book. I should also like to thank Betty Haste, who helped me with the initial draft, painted the watercolours for the mushroom cushion and flower designs, and gave me continuous help and support throughout the writing process.

My grateful thanks also go to MacGregor Designs of Burton-on-Trent for the very generous donation of the firescreen used in the flower section of this book, and to Jane and Bill Greenoff of The Inglestone Collection for the generous gift of the cathedral clock used in the bird section.

I also wish to express my thanks to Jacqueline Kreinik for the interest she has shown in my work and for so generously supplying the full range of Kreinik metallic threads, together with the silk gauze used for the berry design.

I am also grateful to Coats Patons Crafts of Darlington, who provided me with a complete range of Anchor stranded cottons.

Thanks are also due to Adele Bates of Barnyarns for her support and encouragement, and for information about Danish Flower Threads and the Danish Handcraft Guild.

My acknowledgements would not be complete without a very special thank you to Pauline and Anne of the Kaleidoscope needlework and craft materials shop, The Square, Codsall, Staffordshire, who have followed the progress of this book with such interest and have always been at hand with practical help and suggestions.

Finally, I must express my appreciation to friends and neighbours who have been so understanding when I have disappeared for months at a time, while working on this book. Their encouragement has been so much appreciated.

SUPPLIERS

Barnyarns
Langrish
Petersfield,
Hants GU32 1RQ

Coats Patons Crafts
(Customer Liaison)
McMullen Road,
Darlington,
Co Durham DL1 1YQ
Coats Paton will supply information regarding local stockists for Anchor stranded cottons and Kreinik metallic threads.

Framecraft Miniatures Ltd
372/376 Summer Lane,
Hockley,
Birmingham B19 3QA

MacGregor Designs
(The Woodworkers for the Needlecraft World)
PO Box 129,
Burton-on-Trent DE14 3XH

Poppies Needlecrafts
(Mail Order Suppliers)
1 Royal Court,
Leicester Road, Narborough,
Leicester LE9 5EG

The Inglestone Collection
Milton Place,
Circencester Road,
Fairford,
Gloucester GL7 4HR

The photographer would like to offer her grateful thanks to the following people for their loan of locations and props:
The Dining Room Shop, Capt H. Birkbeck, Mr & Mrs M. Mason, Mr G. Mead, Mr & Mrs B. Murray Cox and Mr & Mrs M. Sharland.